Controlling Social Welfare

Controlling Social Welfare

A Sociology of State Welfare Work and Organizations

Christine Cousins
School of Business and Social Sciences
Hatfield Polytechnic

WHEATSHEAF BOOKS · SUSSEX

ST. MARTIN'S PRESS · NEW YORK

First published in Great Britain in 1987 by
WHEATSHEAF BOOKS LTD
A MEMBER OF THE HARVESTER PRESS PUBLISHING GROUP
Publisher: John Spiers
16 Ship Street, Brighton, Sussex
and in the USA by
ST. MARTIN'S PRESS, INC.
175 Fifth Avenue, New York, NY 10010

British Library Cataloguing in Publication Data

Cousins, Christine
    Controlling social welfare: a sociology
    of state welfare work and organisation.
    1. Public welfare   2. Social service
    I. Title
    361   HV40

    ISBN 0-7450-0179-3
    ISBN 0-7450-0400-8 Pbk

Library of Congress Cataloging-in-Publication Data

Cousins, Christine, 1943 –
    Controlling social welfare.

    Bibliography: P.
    Includes index.
    1. Social service – United States.   2. Social
    service – Great Britain.   3. Social workers –
    United States.   4. Social workers – Great Britain
    5. Welfare State.   I. Title.
    HV91.C679   361′.941   87-12851
    ISBN 0-312-01221-7

Typeset in 11 on 12 Times Roman by
Just Words Phototypesetters, Ellen Street, Portslade, Sussex

Printed in Great Britain by Billing & Sons Ltd, Worcester

For Edward, Ben, Matthew, and William

Contents

Contents

Acknowledgements

I wish to express my thanks to my colleagues at Hatfield Polytechnic, especially those in the Sociology group, for their help and encouragement during the period I was writing this book. I should also like to thank the editors at Wheatsheaf Books, for their careful editing, and for making this book possible.

The author and the publisher wish to thank Gower Publishing Company for their kind permission to use material from C. Cousins 'The Labour Process in the State Welfare Sector' in D. Knights and H. Willmott (Eds.) *Managing the Labour Process*, Gower 1986.

Introduction

This book is intended as a contribution to an understanding of the social processes which shape work and divisions of labour within state welfare organizations. Many sociological studies of work concentrate primarily on the most rapidly declining sector of industrial capitalist economies—that of male manual workers in manufacturing industries. But employment in state welfare agencies has been one of the main sources of employment growth in these countries in the post-war period (until economic and political pressures brought a halt in the late 1970s and 1980s), and this growth has been associated with increased female employment as well as increases in non-manual work. The following chapters therefore focus on the implications of the state as employer, of state managerial strategies, of public sector industrial relations, of changes in work processes in state welfare organizations and of the importance of the growth of part-time employment for women in both private and public service industries. Reference is made mainly to Britain and America and to state welfare provision in the health and social services.

A second theme is to examine the nature of the economic, political and ideological pressures which have led to the reorganization of work in state welfare agencies. In the last decade the scope and legitimacy of state welfare provision has increasingly been challenged and has become the source of new political divisions and conflicts. The implications of changing economic and political practices for the organization and control of state welfare work are the focus of later chapters of this book.

The theoretical perspectives and empirical studies discussed in the book are drawn mainly from industrial sociology but also from the work of social theorists on the role of the state in contemporary capitalist societies. Within sociological studies of work and organizations there has in the last decade been a redirection of theoretical concerns prompted by critiques of the dominant structural functionalist paradigm in sociology in the post-war period (for example Burrell and Morgan 1979, Clegg and Dunkerley 1980, Salaman 1978, 1979, Zey Ferrell and Aiken 1981). As the economic and political conditions changed in the 1970s so too did the questions and issues which were addressed within industrial sociology. As Hill (1981) has remarked 'Old concepts were unable to cope with the industrial changes while the new ideas . . . were incompatible with existing approaches'. The sociological study of the work organizations was therefore recast by new approaches which challenged the orthodox and managerially orientated view of organizations as rational, efficient and goal-seeking and called for perspectives which addressed concepts of domination, control and class relations.

These recent perspectives have returned to and developed the central concerns of Marx and Weber in their analysis of work organizations, arguing for the enduring relevance of the insights and approaches of these two theorists (for example Salaman 1978, Burrell and Morgan 1979). Two of the main themes in this literature have been the application of Marx's analysis of the organization and control of the labour process in capitalist production and Weber's work on the process of bureaucratic rationalization as a form of domination. Of particular importance to this redirection was the publication of Braverman's book *Labour and Monopoly Capital* which has since generated an influential labour process debate and a considerable theoretical and empirical literature. The work of Marx on the labour process, and Braverman and the subsequent labour process debate are discussed in Chapter 2. The contribution of Weber to the analysis of contemporary work organization is discussed in Chapter 1.

As we shall see, however, many studies working within the new critical framework do not concern themselves with the labour process in the state service sector. The reason for this is unclear, but it may be related to the theoretical difficulties which are encountered. Braverman and other labour process writers have taken Marx's thesis that the control of labour by employers or their management is necessary for the appropriation of surplus value and therefore profits. The production of state welfare does not produce profits, rather as Burawoy says the state is orientated to 'the provision of social needs' (1985, p.267) and welfare workers cannot therefore be considered as exploited in the same way that workers in the private sector are. This has meant for example that it has been difficult to know how to analyse the class location of state workers, although there have been several attempts to place state workers in theoretical schemes of the class structure, including Carchedi (1977), Crompton and Gubbay (1977), and Wright (1976).

These writers have argued that the work and employment conditions of state and private sector workers are similar, since the labour of both is controlled and supervised by management. In their analysis of state labour processes they consider that state managers are guided by principles of productivity and cost efficiency and constrained to act as private sector managers in order to contain costs. As Wright (1985) notes with reference to his own scheme, however, the problem with this approach is that the concept of class relations, of both private and state workers, rests almost exclusively on relations of domination of one group by another rather than on the concept of exploitation.

Some of these theoretical problems can be overcome to an extent by considering the views of the critical writers, Habermas and Offe who, in conjunction with O'Connor, argue that state provision of welfare is a form of production which not only reproduces capitalist social relations but also negates them by introducing new, and additional social relations of production. In Chapter 3 we therefore argue that the critical theorists have important insights to offer in their consideration of the contradictory role which states have to sustain. The critical theorists consider that, unlike the private sector, state welfare organizations are not governed by the logic of maximizing profits, although they are dependent on the revenues derived from profits and the prosperity of the private sector. In the absence of market criteria, decisions in the state sector take place in the context of a diffusion of objectives and pressures in public policy making as well as budgetary constraints. Moreover the different economic and political demands may be non-commensurate and have contradictory effects.

A few studies, for example Batstone *et al.* (1984) on the Post Office, Child (1984) on the introduction of information technology in service industries and Ferner (1985) on British Rail, have used this theoretical approach to demonstrate that the different mode of rationality, or to use Batstone's term 'political contingencies' in the public sector has consequences for the strategies adopted by management, trade unions, and workers.

The state welfare sector contains one of the largest concentrations of women, migrant and part-time workers in low-paid and low-status jobs. In Chapter 4 we examine the contributions of recent theories of the labour process, industrial reserve army of labour and the operations of labour markets to the analysis of sexual and racial divisions of labour. Here an important contribution has come from feminist writers who have argued that it is not only employers' strategies which have shaped the ways in which women have been drawn into the paid labour force in the post-war period, but also relations of gender based on sexual divisions in the home and the familial ideology embodied in it. The forms that women's employment patterns have taken in the post-war period, especially in the state welfare sector, are also considered.

Professional provider groups also constitute an important part of the workforce in welfare organizations. Some professional occupations retain considerable degrees of technical autonomy, the ability to determine the content, terms and conditions of their employment, a role in policy making, and the ability to define clients' needs and treatments. Their work processes cannot necessarily be seen as analogous to those of industrial workers nor subject to the deskilling and loss of technique that Braverman and others have described as central to the proletarianization of industrial wage workers. Several writers however have argued that these professional and higher-level workers are, like the semi-professional and predominantly feminized occupations, now vulnerable to the extension of managerial controls and are undergoing an incipient form of proletarianization. Chapter 5 examines the conflicting views on the changing nature of professional and higher-level work and on the strategies of professionalism pursued by the aspiring professional occupations. The technical and sexual divisions of labour between welfare professionals, and the social processes which have shaped these divisions, are also considered. Important here are corporate alliances between the state and some professional provider groups which have led to the selective privileging and sponsorship of these groups and the pursuit of that sponsorship by other occupations.

Chapter 6 examines the emergence and militancy of public sector trade unions in the USA and the UK within the theoretical framework of a sector model developed by the critical writers. Using this model it is argued that it is possible to distinguish the relationship between workers in the public and private sectors, as well as economic and ideological conflicts of interest between workers in each sector. In both America and Britain public sector unions were implicated in the fiscal crises of governments in the mid-1970s, and in subsequent attempts by governments to restrict the growth of public expenditure and public employment. These developments contributed to the conditions in the late 1970s in which ideological shifts to the right, and the political realignments which supported them, took place. In the 1980s a new dimension was therefore added to the restructuring of welfare work by specific ideological and political practices of the new right.

The sources of influence on the Reagan and Conservative administrations, and the set of policies which have been directed to welfare work in the 1980s, are discussed in Chapter 7. However, it is also argued that in the context of diffuse and conflicting economic and political pressures operating on state management the implementation of government policies has incompatible and contradictory consequences for governments, managers and workers. The effects of different government policies on welfare work are examined with respect to health care in the USA and to the NHS and social services in Britain.

A number of themes discussed in earlier chapters are developed in Chapter 8 through two case studies of the implementation of recent government policies in the NHS in Britain. The first case study considers the initial effects of the introduction of new management structures based on private sector principles, whilst the second examines the imposition of a programme of privatization of ancillary services in the NHS.

This book is intended primarily to serve as a textbook and this has necessarily meant a discussion of basic information in some areas. However, the extensive literature on the different aspects of the topics discussed has also inevitably meant that some important theoretical and substantive issues are only briefly mentioned, although I refer the reader to the main references where possible. There is for example no exposition of the debate on class relations and class formation and the difficult problem already referred to of the class location of state workers. It would seem that there is a theoretical gap in the literature here that has yet to be filled. There is also less discussion of racial divisions of labour than I would have liked, as this constitutes a significant part of the composition of the state welfare workforce. The following discussion is also limited in its reference to policy areas outside the health and social services and to welfare policy developments in countries other than Britain and America.

1 Weber and the Sociology of Organizations

Max Weber's discussion of bureaucracy has often been taken as a starting point for the sociological study of organizations. His ideas and the subsequent debate have exerted a wide-ranging influence on the study of modern organizations. More recently however there has been a plea to return to the macro sociological concerns of Weber and his attempt to place the concept of bureaucracy within the context of the process of rationalization, the emergence of industrial capitalism and types of domination.

These themes in Weber's work are discussed in the first section of this chapter. In the second and third parts of the chapter we discuss the ways in which Weber's ideas were developed and interpreted and the dominance of a view of organizations as rational structures designed to maximize efficiency in the achievement of goals. The critiques of this orthodox model reformulated organizational analysis in the 1970s and 1980s, and at the end of this chapter we discuss recent and alternative perspectives of organizations.

WEBER, RATIONALITY AND BUREAUCRACY

One of the major themes in Weber's work was the subjection of the Western world to the process of rationalization. This process was Weber's 'personal vision' (Freund 1968) and he analysed its fate in all human activities; religion, law, art, science, music, politics and economics. By rationalization he meant, as Wrong describes 'the process by which explicit, abstract, intellectual, calculable rules and procedures are increasingly substituted for sentiment, tradition and rule of thumb' (1970 p.26). For Weber rationalization demystifies and instrumentalizes life: 'It means that there are no mysterious incalculable forces that come into play but rather that one can, in principle, master all things by calculation' (Weber 1948, p.139).

Weber does not view rationalization as some metaphysical force but 'it relates to the meaning which men attach to their activities' (Freund 1968). In this way Weber was able to show in his book *The Protestant Ethic and the Spirit of Capitalism* that the asceticism of the early protestants was one of the factors influencing the rationality of economic activity and hence contributed to the emergence and mode of organization of modern capitalism.

Types of Rationality
A clearer understanding of Weber's notion of rationalization can be obtained by examining his ideal types of social action. In his *Economy and Society* he intended to develop a scheme in which rational forms of action could be compared with irrational or emotional or traditional forms. Weber distinguished four types of social action, that is 'human conduct orientated to the behaviour of others'; First, in purposive rational action an individual rationally assesses the probable results of a given act in terms of the calculation of means to an end. Secondly, in value rational action an individual orientates his planned or calculated action to the achievement of ultimate values or ideals, for example, equality, justice or duty. Thirdly, affectual action is determined by the emotional states of feeling of the actor, for example anger or love. Fourthly, traditional action occurs through the habituation of long practice, governed by custom.

The first two types of rational action led Weber to distinguish between formal and substantive rationality, a distinction which underlies much of his discussion of the sociology of economic life. Formal rationality consists of the rational calculation of the most adequate means of achieving given ends. Such rational calculations could be expressed in numerical or technical terms, such as accounting or cost-benefit analysis, and give information as to the best methods to be chosen for specific ends. Formal rationality, therefore, refers to the calculation of means. Substantive rationality on the other hand involves 'a relation to the absolute values or to the content of the particular given ends to which it is orientated' (1947, p.185). Substantive rationality, then, relates to ultimate values, and it is from this point of view that the outcome of action can be judged. As we discuss later, Weber considered that formal rationality was incompatible with and in conflict with substantive rationality and that the application of formal rationality could undermine or even subvert the substantive ends of social organizations.

Formal Rationality and Economic Organization

For Weber an essential aspect of modern capitalism was the development of formally rational organizations, orientated to calculative methods of 'capital-accounting'.[1] A high level of calculability within the organization was required, Weber maintained, by the 'capitalist market economy which demands the official business of administration be discharged precisely, unambiguously, continuously, with as much speed as possible.' The unpredictability and instability of economic markets and technological innovation required a stable and calculative form of organizational control and discipline. Such an organization gave management a superior bargaining position with regard to labour markets, commodity markets and its command over capital and credit.

The organization which according to Weber carried out the most rationally 'known means of imperative control over human beings' was bureaucracy. 'It thus makes possible a particularly high degree of calculability of results for the heads of the organizations' (p.337). But although bureaucracy is fostered by capitalist rationality and in turn promotes it, is also a form of administration to be found in all large-scale modern organizations. '[It] is true of church, and state, of armies, political parties, economic enterprises, organizations to promote all kinds of causes, private associations, clubs and many others' (p.337).

Bureaucracy and Legitimacy

Weber places his discussion of bureaucracy within an historical and comparative analysis of 'structures of dominancy', in which different organizational forms are related to different authority structures. The defining characteristic of an organization for Weber was the presence of a leader and administrative staff whose action is orientated to a set of beliefs governing authority. Such beliefs make it probable that commands from a leader, or an individual in a position of authority, will be obeyed. Different forms of belief, that is different types of legitimate authority, of which Weber distinguished charismatic, traditional and rational legal,[2] are associated with different organizational structures. Of particular interest to us is rational legal authority which is associated with bureaucratic administration.

Weber therefore stressed forms of domination in terms of beliefs about the legitimacy of power, not as in Marx's writing in terms of economic relations. In rational legal authority, beliefs about the validity of such authority rested, according to Weber, on ideas that the authority was applicable to everyone, and that the rules were based on abstract and impersonal principles. With respect to the structure of bureaucracy Weber lists eight elements which refer to a continuous task organization, a specialized division of labour, hierarchy, work regulated by rules, and written rules and communications[3]. Weber also lists the criteria for the appointment of a bureaucratic staff: separation from the means of production or administration, selection on the basis of qualifications, a career with promotion prospects and subjection to control and discipline[4] (Weber 1947, pp.329-34; see also Albrow 1970).

Weber's concept of rational legal bureaucracy is an ideal-type, that is, an abstraction and accentuation of only selected aspects of a social phenomenon, which although found in reality are rarely discovered in this specific form. In constructing this ideal-type Weber was concerned to contrast bureaucratic and non-bureaucratic forms and to link them with his thesis of rationalization as the dominant tendency of modern Western history. It is the element of formal rational calculability which distinguishes bureaucracy from other forms of organization and makes it indispensable to the requirements of modern capitalism.

Whilst Weber was able to point to the essential increase in rational bureaucracy through its complete indispensability, he left open the question of bureaucratic power. Bureaucratic officials are able to increase their power still further through special knowledge and expertise, and access to information and secrets. According to Weber 'The power position of a fully developed bureaucracy is always great, under normal conditions overtowering. The political "master" always finds himself *vis à vis* the trained official, in the position of a dilettante facing the expert'. A central question for Weber was 'Who controls the bureaucracy?' and what checks or limitations existed to limit its power. He considered several mechanisms whereby democratic control could be exerted over bureaucratic authority to oppose directly the bureaucratic tendency; these were collegiality, the separation of powers, amateur administration, direct democracy and representation (1947, pp.392-423).

Weber was aware, however, that capitalist economic activity and its associated forms of rational bureaucracy were based on 'irrational' foundations. The structures of control and discipline established in such organizations contravened substantive human values, for example, 'benevolent relationships or 'individual creativity and autonomy of action'. 'Such absolute depersonalisation is contrary to all elementary forms of human relationships' (1968, p.637). Rational economic activity held for Weber an unavoidable element of irrationality in which formal calculative rationality pushed out substantive value rationality, promoting deprivation and unfreedom. Human action had, in Weber's view, unintentional consequences; action intended as a means to an end becomes an end in itself. Thus, technically rational rules and procedures, set up as means, become independent, separated from their purposes, an end in themselves. 'Structures originally set up by man, now in their turn, encompass and determine him like an iron-cage' (Loewith 1970).

Weber perceived the rational calculation of work as dehumanizing 'the performance of each individual worker is mathematically measured, each man becomes a little cog in a machine'. Loewith (1970) has pointed out that Weber himself saw his pessimistic view of the meaningless irrationality which rules over men as similar to Marx's concept of alienation. For Weber, however, it was alienation from all modern institutions and cultural activities that were subject to the process of bureaucratic rationality, and not as Marx saw alienation as a product of capitalist social relations and mode of production. Consequently, Weber thought socialism would extend the requirements for formal bureaucratization, increasing the irrationality of economic and social life.

Weber's concept of bureaucracy is, therefore, associated with his fatalistic view of the advance of rationalization. He was able to demonstrate how a particular kind of rationality was incorporated into a form of organization, which in consequence became a 'structure of dominancy' over people that they, themselves, had created.

Subsequent treatments of Weber's views have, however, followed two very different strands of intellectual thought. First, there has been the development of a sociology of organizations in which Weber's ideal type of bureaucracy has been interpreted as a rational organization designed to maximize efficiency in the achievement of its goals. This interpretation is discussed in the next section. Secondly, critical theorists, a group of writers associated with the Frankfurt school, have shared Weber's view (although not his fatalism) of the increasing rationalization of modern capitalist society and of the way in which formal technical rationality becomes a form of domination of means over ends. Important here has been Habermas's (1971) concept of 'technocratic consciousness' as an ideology of technical rationality which conceals the pursuit of particular class interests (the ideas of the critical theorists are discussed in Chapter 3).

CRITICS OF WEBER

Stemming from Weber's work on bureaucracy has been a large number of empirical studies of bureaucratic organizations. From a functionalist perspective, the dominant sociological theory until the 1960s, each of these studies challenged aspects of Weber's work. Three such criticisms are discussed here: first a rejection of Weber's claim that rational bureaucracy is capable of achieving the highest degree of efficiency; secondly the claim that Weber confused two sources of authority; and thirdly, a rejection of the empirical validity of Weber's ideal type.

(i) In the first case, many writers have assumed that Weber, in his description of bureaucracy, equated rationality with efficiency. Thus, Mouzelis (1967) avers that 'an ideally rational organization in the Weberian sense is an organization performing its tasks with maximum efficiency'. Blau (1970) sees Weber as presenting 'an implicit functional analysis of the interdependence between the characteristics of bureaucracy, with rational efficient administration as the criteria of function'. As a consequnce several writers have documented the ways in which the elements of Weber's bureaucracy lead, in fact, to inefficiency rather than efficiency. So, for example, in a famous essay, Merton (1952) argued that an emphasis on abstract rules and impersonality between officials and clients can have the 'unintended consequences' of red tape and officiousness. Blau in *The Dynamics of Bureaucracy* has shown how administrative efficiency was often better achieved when members of a law enforcement agency used unofficial and informal practices.

These studies were, as Albrow notes, celebrating the discovery in the 1930s of informal work groups and applying these insights to the study of administration. As such they were seeking to offer a corrective to Weber's view that rational bureaucracy leads to a maximum of stability, precision, calculability and efficiency. However, as Albrow (1970) has further argued, these writers were mistaken to asume that Weber equated rationality with efficiency, a point which is taken up later in this chapter. Moreover, as we have already seen, an emphasis on formal rationality was, for Weber, unlikely to lead to the achievement of substantive rationality, 'indeed the most perfect formal system might operate to defeat the purposes and values which animated it' (Albrow p.64).

(ii) A second criticism, initially made by Parsons (1947) and later taken up by Gouldner and others, concerns the claim that Weber's ideal type of bureaucracy confused two sources of authority. In Parsons' opinion, Weber confused two essentially different types of social structure, firstly, authority based on incumbency of office, that is, bureaucratic position and secondly, authority based on professional knowledge or technical expertise. The latter stems from Weber's statement that 'Bureaucratic administration means fundamentally the exercise of control on the basis of knowledge'.

Gouldner in his study *Patterns of Industrial Bureaucracy* (1954) showed that the different sources of authority either generated or thwarted the emergence of consent. Thus, Gouldner was able to demonstrate that consent to bureaucratic authority was problematic, as the imposition of rules by either management or workers involved conflict and tension. In contrast, rules emanating from technical experts were seen as legitimate and their imposition entailed little conflict. In Gouldner's view, Weber saw 'authority as given consent because it was legitimate rather than being legitimate because it evoked consent. For Weber therefore consent is always a datum to be taken for granted, rather than a problem whose sources had to be traced' (p.223).

Other writers too have differentiated between types of organization based on bureaucratic authority on the one hand and professional or technical authority on the other. Stinchcombe (1959) for example, in an analysis of the American building industry, argued that there is a distinction between organizations based on rational bureaucratic principles (the Weberian model) and those based on craft principles as in the building industry. Burns and Stalker (1961) made a famous distinction between 'mechanistic' (Weberian) management structures and 'organic' management structures; the latter having delegated and decentralized decision-making structures and a flexible and changing division of labour.[5]

(iii) A third criticism of Weber's ideal-type bureaucracy has focused on the empirical validity of his model. Blau and Scott (1963) have claimed that the actual characteristics of bureaucratic structures and their contribution to administrative efficiency is a matter for empirical investigation rather than definition. Organizational analysts who have followed this approach have since devoted much attention to discovering empirically how and why different organizations have different structures. The Aston University studies[6] for example, have criticised the Weberian model as a unitary concept of bureaucracy. Instead of assuming that an organization either is, or is not, bureaucratic, the Aston researchers argue that it is more useful to regard organizations as ranging from more to less bureaucratic in their activities. Bureaucracy is not then a unitary concept, but organizations can be bureaucratic in a number of ways, along several dimensions. After specifying the dimensions of organizational structure, the Aston research team was able to construct profiles of different organizational structures, which could then be related to aspects of the organization's context (for example, size, technology, type and stability of environment) and its performance (extent to which goals are achieved)[7].

THE ORTHODOX SOCIOLOGICAL MODEL OF ORGANIZATIONS

Although organizational analysis is renowned for its diversity of perspectives it is possible to speak of a dominant paradigm or model which underlies the diverse conceptual schemes. This model is here called the 'orthodox' sociological model of organizations, although other writers have labelled it the 'dominant', (Zey Ferrell and Aiken 1981), the 'conventional' (Salaman 1978), the 'rational' (Benson 1981) or 'goal' (Georgiou 1981) paradigms of organizational analysis.

In the last decade the orthodox model has itself been the subject of substantial criticism. A first critique, from a social action perspective, has centred on the methodological conceptions of organizations, a second more recent critique has focused on the neglect of a theory of power and the institutional context within which organizations operate. The first of these critiques, the action critique, will not be presented here since it has been extensively discussed elsewhere (for example Burrell and Morgan 1979, Clegg and Dunkerley 1980, Silverman 1970). Below however we consider some of the ways in which the sociology of organizations has been reformulated through perspectives derived from the social action approach, namely, the concept of negotiated order and the need to understand social structures as produced through the actions of human agents.

In this chapter we concentrate on the second of these critiques, in which it was argued by a number of writers that the study of organizations had become narrowly focused on the internal structural arrangements of organizations, isolated from their wider societal and historical context. Theory had been constructed which reified organizational goals and promoted an overly rational image of the functioning of organizations. Power relations—domination, exploitation, control and coercion—were seldom analysed in the orthodox approach. Furthermore many studies, although formulated in the name of Weber, had taken his thesis out of context and misconceived and distorted his intention. As a consequence organizational analysis was accused of being 'static and formalistic', 'ethno-centric, non-historical and microscopic', and of 'being locked into an acceptance of managerially defined problems' (Allen 1975, Burrell and Morgan 1979, Clegg and Dunkerley 1980, Eldridge and Crombie 1974, Mouzelis 1967, Salaman 1978, Zey Ferrell and Aiken 1981).

The critique of the substantive content of the orthodox model of organizations included, therefore, ideologically conservative assumptions, the reification of organizational goals, the overly rational image of organizations and the inadequate attention given to power and class relations in organizational studies (see Zey Ferrell and Aiken 1981 and Burrell and Morgan 1979 for a more detailed critique of the orthodox model). The following discussion examines two themes which were particularly pervasive in the orthodox model: the importance attached to organizational goals, and the view that organizations are rationally determined structures for the efficient pursuit of these goals.

Organizational Goals

An important element of the orthodox sociological model is that organizations are conceived as social units deliberately set up to achieve specific goals. Etzioni (1964), Blau and Scott (1963), Parsons (1958), Selznick (1949) and in Britain the Brunel Institute for Organization and Social Studies[8] have all defined organizations as social units which pursue specific goals. Clearly, most organizations have at some point in the past been deliberately set up for a purpose and have a founding charter, constitution or set of aims and it is this purposive creation which is used to distinguish organizations from other social groups. As Clegg and Dunkerley point out 'organizations . . . comprise planned and coordinated activities. Since these do not occur randomly there must be some agreed upon basis for them' (1980, p.317).

However, important as the goal concept has been in organizational theory, many writers have noted that it presents difficulties as a tool of analysis. The goals of an organization are often vague, multiple or conflicting and this is especially so in welfare organizations. But even if organizational goals are less vague and more explicit, as for instance in private business firms, there may be disagreements as to the means of attaining them. Organizational goals can also change over time and can be displaced, so that organizations pursue goals other than those they were originally set up to achieve (Michels 1962). Moreover, the goal model involves a form of reification and personification, that is the imputing to abstract entities the qualities of concrete units or human characteristics. Only people have goals and motivations, not organizations (Silverman 1970).

A more useful perspective, which writers such as Crozier (1964), Perrow (1979) and Strauss (1963), have suggested, is to view the actual outcome of organizational work as the result of the activity of many different participants; each with a different occupation, training, interests and goals. Organizational structure is then the outcome of negotiation, conflict and bargaining between these individuals and groups at the different organizational levels. This may well result in a discrepancy between the stated or official goals of the organization, and the real or operative goals.

Perrow (1961) sees operative goals as 'the ends to be sought through the actual operating principles of the organization which tells us what the organization is actually trying to do regardless of what the official goals say are the aims'. Furthermore the operative goals are shaped by the dominant group; goals therefore refer to the outcome of the activities and policies of one particular group. Perrow's approach is useful since it directs attention to the way in which organizations can be used by groups within it to attain their own private ends. Like Strauss, whose work is discussed below, the emphasis is on organizational processes and the policies and aims that emerge from the activities of different organizational groups. However, as we discuss below and in Chapters 2 and 3, this pluralist approach tends to ignore the structural constraints which operate on organizational members, whether this be the economic constraints of profit making in the private sector, or the different economic and political constraints implicit in the management of state organizations.

The Overly Rational Image of Organizations
A second element in the orthodox sociological model of organizations is the view that organizations have rationally planned and co-ordinated activities, that is, structures, to achieve their goals. But this view assumes a tighter fit between structure, processes and goals than many studies suggest. As mentioned above, several writers have argued that organizational structures are the outcome of a political process of conflict, bargaining and negotiation between different groups and coalitions. There is then not one rationality but a multiplicity of rationalities originating from the various groups and coalitions in the organization. From these internal struggles a dominant coalition will emerge and attempt to impose its own ends on organizational policy. The orthodox sociological model thus avoids the questions of whose rationality becomes or is pre-eminent. But the policies of the dominant coalition may not always be implemented: they may be resisted, or subverted by other groups in the organization, or have unintended consequences. (The implications of this for the concept of managerial strategy are discussed in the next chapter.)

In the orthodox model of organizations there is an assumption that it is possible to devise organizational structures which best fit or are most efficient in the achievement of stated goals. Such an approach for example underlies the work of the Brunel Institute for Organization and Social Studies, which was influential in devising 'appropriate' structures for Social

Service Departments and the National Health Service in Britain in the 1970s. Here there was an intention to devise the necessary conditions for the most efficient and effective methods of administration and an assumption that this is in accord with a rationally planned organization. (See Chapter 3 for an alternative view of the formulation of 'appropriate' organizational structures for state welfare organizations.)

Critics of this orthodox model have however questioned the concept of the most efficient means of production or administration as value-laden. Rather they have argued that the concept of efficiency is not neutral or apolitical, and cannot be divorced from the issue of efficient for whom or for what? Rueschemeyer has argued that the question 'efficient for which interest' can be answered only by reference to power. Hence 'It is the most powerful interests that determine which efficiency criteria will select among different forms of division of labour and thus shape the particular forms of social production and reproduction' (1986, p.171). The concept of efficiency can therefore be used in ways which mask the interests and purposes of organizational designs of the dominant group within the organization. The view that organizations are rational structures set up to achieve their goals in the most efficient way has been legitimated, Albrow has claimed on the erroneous assumption that Weber associated rationality with efficiency. It is to this discussion that we now turn.

Rationality and Efficiency in Weber's Work

Albrow has argued that the real relation between rationality and efficiency in Weber's work can best be understood by considering the means by which efficiency is commonly measured, 'through the calculation of costs in money terms or in time or energy expended. Such calculations are formal procedures which do not themselves guarantee efficiency, but are amongst the conditions for determining what level of efficiency has been reached' (1970 p.65).

Weber's notion of a formally rational bureaucracy was one that involved calculative procedures and their application as technical rules by experts. It was an organization which carried out the 'most rationally known means (that is, calculated, technical rules) of imperative control over human beings', for the purpose of 'establishing stringent discipline, precision and reliability within the organization' (Weber 1947, p.337). Instead, then, of efforts at efficiency, 'there are efforts at "efficiency of control" which demand some form of power over reluctant parties'. 'For Weber the rationalities, the modes of calculation, of managerial elites were the main mechanism shaping the actual use of power' (McNeil 1981, pp.50, 53).

Weber was aware that such formal rational procedures did not necessarily result in the achievement of the ends or purposes of the organization. In fact, as discussed earlier, he was concerned with the 'paradox of consequences', when the use of rational procedures has irrational consequences. Weber therefore did not argue that the consequences of formal rationality had to be rational 'only that consequences had to be traced back to modes of calculation in the heads of managerial elites' (McNeil 1981, p.54). The most important aspect of Weber's work was that he was able to link organizations as structures of dominancy and control with the legitimizing ideas and values (i.e. 'rationality' or 'efficiency') of these elites and of the wider society.

SOCIAL PROCESSES AND LOGICS OF ACTION

Lastly in this chapter we examine perspectives of organizational activity which see organizational structures as emerging from the actions, interactions, negotiations and conflict between different groups and individuals rather than a view of organizational structures as the result of deliberate and rational planning in order to achieve a specific goal. In the first of these perspectives the emphasis is on processes within organizations as continually emerging through the actions and interactions of their members; here the work of Strauss on negotiated order theory and the arguments of Giddens on the problematic of structure and action are discussed. The second approach is to be found in the work of Karpik, which represents an attempt to link micro level analysis of interactions between organizational actors to historical and economic contexts.

The perspective that has made 'negotiation' the key concept in organizational analysis is that of Strauss and his colleagues (1963, 1978). In their research into a psychiatric hospital, 'physicians, residents, interns, nurses, aides, social workers, administrators, nutritionists, clerical personnel' were all 'ostensibly working toward the primary goal of the organization which is to make the patient well' (Day and Day 1977, p.129). All these groups have 'different types of training, professional socialisation, experience . . . personal backgrounds . . . and occupy quite different hierarchical positions in the hospital (Day and Day 1979, p.129). There are thus a multitude of different perspectives, often conflicting, regarding patient care and conceptions of the etiology and treatment of mental illness, not only between the groups but also within them. The few general rules of the hospital were inadequate to solve these conflicting perspectives and anyway could be, as Strauss remarked 'stretched, negotiated, argued, as well as ignored or applied at convenient moments' (1983, p.153). As a consequence, an informal 'negotiated order' emerged in which the actual working arrangements were the result of pacts, contracts, bargaining and understandings within and between groups. Such negotiations had a temporal limit and eventually would be 'reviewed, re-evaluated, revised, revoked or renewed'.

Organizational structures are, therefore, seldom stable and are continually emerging through the actions and interactions of individuals and groups. For Strauss an organizational goal is no more than a 'generalised mandate' or 'symbolic referent' the sense of which is continuously re-interpreted and re-worked through local and day-to-day negotiations.

In their critical review of negotiated order theory Day and Day find that it presents 'an interactional model involving a processual and emergent analysis of the manner in which the division of labour and work are accomplished in large organizations' (1977, p.126). Yet despite these insights the perspective has a number of weaknesses, the most serious of which 'is the overall failure to place specific negotiating processes within their total contextual framework' (p.135). As a consequence negotiated order theorists 'fail to critically

examine the hard realities of power and politics and the
influence they exert' (p.134). In his more recent work, however, Strauss has attempted to meet these criticisms by incor-
porating an analysis of the ' structural context' within which
negotiations take place, and the 'structural properties' of
social settings.

Drawing on the work of social action theorists, including
Strauss, but also the work of Silverman (1970), Zimmerman
(1969) Bittner (1965) and others[9], organizations can be
viewed as processual, as continually emerging through the
actions of their members as they actively interpret and pursue
their own interests and aims. Organizations cannot therefore
be conceived as having structures, functions or goals which
operate independently of the social activities and interactions
of their members. As Giddens has said, 'institutions do not
just work "behind the backs" of the social actors who produce
and reproduce them' (1982, p.37).

Berger and Luckman (1966) have discussed the dialectical
process by which people construct a social order through their
'ongoing out-pouring . . . of physical and mental activity' and
yet regard the product of that activity as a reality that exists
independently of themselves. The social order involves both
subjective human activity and objective social structure, men
produce society and are produced by it, 'the product acts back
upon the producer.'

A conception of social structure, then, has to incorporate
an understanding of the continual production and reproduction of human activity and the meanings which are given to
that activity. As Abrams (1982) has argued, sociologists need
to understand the 'puzzle of human agency'. One attempt to
theorize the 'problematic of action and structure' has been
that of Giddens (1979), who has suggested the concept of
structuration for the dialectical process whereby structures
come into being through the continuous activities of human
beings across time and space. To put it another way, social
structures are seen as produced by human agency and yet are
the very medium through which this production takes place.
This production necessarily involves 'capable, conscious,
knowing' agents who may act not simply to reconstitute the
structure but to transform it. Giddens' conception of action

involves human agents as both knowledgeable and capable. He defines 'capability' as 'making a difference' of 'intervening in the world so as to influence events'. Knowledgeability is defined as the application of tactic knowledge to secure autonomy in the course of everyday life'. Knowledgeability includes for Giddens the reasons people have for their actions, 'the rationalization of action' which is the 'chronic reflexive monitoring of conduct that social actors routinely carry on', and is 'involved with how these actions are sustained.'

A similar notion to 'rationalizations of action' is Karpik's use of 'logics of actions' as the basic analytical tool in the study of organizations. Karpik defines logics of action as the 'observed rationalities of organizational actors and coalitions from the point of view of an outside observer, e.g. a re-searcher'. Logics of action are the 'principles of action around which individuals and groups organize their attitudes and behaviour' (Karpik 1981, p.397). Hence, for Karpik, there is no one rationality, but forms of rationality which he calls 'logics of action'.

One way of relating structure and actions is, therefore, to start from a bottom up approach as Karpik does, in which the forms of rationality or 'logics of action' of individuals, groups, coalitions are mobilized as strategies. Karpik sees organ-izations as political processes, in which through bargaining, negotiation and conflict, coalitions compete for power. A dominant coalition emerges which seeks to impose its own logic of action on other organizational groups. Important however, is Karpik's attempt to locate 'logics of action' within an historical analysis of forms of capitalism 'that serve as the sources of power and rules of competition used by corpora-tions to control production processes, markets and clientele' (Weiss 1981, p.394). Hence the 'logics of action are not arbitrary . . . [but] organizational coalitions choose pre-ferences that are historically and economically conditioned' (Weiss 1981, p.394).

CONCLUSION

Bureaucracy for Weber was the most rationally 'known means of imperative control over human beings'. He demonstrated how a particular kind of formal or technical rationality became incorporated in a form of organization which in turn became a structure of dominancy and control over people. The calculative procedures and technical rules of bureaucratic organizations were the main mechanisms which enabled organizational elites to shape the actual use of power (McNeil 1981). However, as we have seen, the subsequent development of organizational sociology has had a limited interpretation of Weber's work.

Critiques of this orthodox model of organizations have in the 1970s and 1980s reformulated the study of organizations to take into account the internal political processes and structures of control that emerge through the activities and beliefs of organizational members and have linked these to external power relations. As Salaman has noted, critics of the orthodox model have followed Weber and Marx in their rejection of 'the widely prevalent view that organizational structure follows from the application of neutral apolitical priorities—such as efficiency, technology etc.—and insisted that such concepts should be exposed for their political purposes and assumptions'. They have instead 'stressed that organizational structure—the design of work and control— can only be seen in terms of general processes of organizational control initiated by, and in the interests of, those who ran or dominated the organization' (Salaman 1978, p.539).

NOTES

1. The maximum of formal rationality of capital-accounting rested, Weber believed, on a number of conditions. Foremost amongst these was the existence of formally free labour, freedom of the labour market, and freedom of selection of workers. Labour is formally free in the sense, that is, of not being slaves who are purchased and maintained for a lifetime, but are nevertheless a class who are compelled to sell their labour in order to live. Secondly, the complete

appropriation of ownership and control of the means of production, which means that there must be no workers' rights to participate in management, or control access to jobs, or appropriate the product. Such conditions impede the achievement of maximum formal rationality. However, 'Free labour and the complete appropriation of the means of production create the most favourable conditions for discipline' (1947, p.248).

2. In distinguishing between power and authority Weber sees power as the probability that one actor within a social relationship will be able to carry out his will despite resistance. Authority, however, exists when obedience to commands rests on a belief in the legitimacy of those commands, a belief that the orders are justified and it is right to obey.

     Weber distinguished three 'ideal types' of legitimate authority:

     (1) Rational legal—a belief in the 'legality' of patterns of normative rules, and the right of those who occupy positions of authority under such rules to issue commands. Obedience is owed to the legally established impersonal order and extends to persons exercising authority only by virtue of their incumbency of office and the formal legality of commands.

     (2) Traditional—a belief in the rightness and appropriateness of traditional ways of doing things; subjects obey out of personal loyalty or respect to persons occupying traditional status.

     (3) Charismatic—rests on extraordinary personal qualities and deeds of a charismatic leader.

3. Weber formulated eight propositions about the structure of rational legal authority systems which following Albrow (1970) can be stated thus:

     (1) Official tasks are organized on a continuous regulated basis.

     (2) These tasks are divided into functionally distinct spheres each of which is furnished with the requisite authority and sanctions.

     (3) Offices are arranged hierarchically, the rights of control and complaint between them being specified.

     (4) The rules according to which work is conducted may be either technical or legal. In both cases trained persons are necessary.

     (5) The resources of the organization are quite distinct from those of the members as private individuals.

     (6) The office holder cannot appropriate his office.

     (7) Administration is based on written documents and this tends to make the office (Bureau) the hub of the modern organization.

     (8) Legal authority systems can take many forms, but are seen at their purest in a bureaucratic administrative staff.

4. Weber viewed the purest type of exercise of legal authority as that which employs a bureaucratic administrative staff, who are appointed and function according to the following criteria:

     (1) They are personally free and subject to authority only with respect to their impersonal official obligations.

     (2) They are organized in a clearly defined hierarchy of offices.

(3) Each office has a clearly defined sphere of competence in the legal sense.

(4) The office is filled by a free contractual relationship. Thus, in principle, there is free selection.

(5) Candidates are selected on the basis of technical qualifications . . . and are appointed not elected.

(6) They are remunerated by fixed salaries in money, with a right to pensions.

(7) The office is treated as the sole, or at least primary, occupation of the incumbent.

(8) It constitutes a career. There is a system of 'promotion' according to seniority or achievement or both. Promotion is dependent upon the judgement of superiors.

(9) The official works entirely separated from ownership of the means of administration and without appropriation of his position.

(10) He is subject to strict and systematic discipline and control in the conduct of his office.

5. In welfare organizations the contrast between professional and bureaucratic modes of organization, or mechanistic and organic modes, has been seen as particularly important. Social Service Departments, hospitals, schools and universities have been said to comprise two conflicting and separate structures, administrative hierarchies and professional collegiate groups. Writers such as G. Smith (1970) and Blau (1963) have considered that each organizational mode is appropriate to particular circumstances and conditions, so that professional or organic modes of organization are seen as more appropriate to the delivery of welfare services, whilst bureaucracy distorts and constrains effective work with clients. These views were highlighted in the early 1970s in discussions of how the new Seebohm Social Service Departments might be organized. Several advocates proposed that the new department be organized in organic or polyarchic modes, in which professional social work practices and client-orientated policies evolved from flexible, participatory and non-hierarchical management structures. In the event, however, hierarchic management structures developed in most social service departments. Instrumental in promoting the hierarchic principle was the research team at the Brunel Institute for Organization and Social Studies (BIOSS), who considered that there was no inconsistency between social work professionalism and management hierarchy, but rather that social workers were best organized in explicitly defined management hierarchies.

6. See for example Pugh and Hickson (1976).

7. This approach, which has become known as 'contingency theory', has been able to establish statistical relationships between organizational characteristics, but the approach has been largely descriptive and has not been without its critics. Amongst the most influential criticisms have been those made by Child (1972) who argues that contingency theory is inadequate because 'it fails to give due attention to the

agency of choice by whoever have the power to direct the organization'. It is the 'strategic choices' made by the dominant coalition which lead to the design of organizational structures, within the constraints of organizational activity, size and environment. By the dominant coalition Child means those who collectively hold most power over a period of time, not necessarily those who hold formally designated authoritative positions in the organization.

8. See for example Rowbottom *et al.* (1974) and Jacques (1978).
9. See also G. Salaman and K. Thompson (1973), and A. J. Elger, 'Industrial Organizations' in J. B. Mckinlay (ed.) (1975).

2 Marx, Braverman and the Labour Process Debate

Marx's analysis of the capitalist labour process and its subsequent development by contemporary writers is the theme of this chapter. In recent years the insights of Marx have, like those of Weber, been seen to be of increasing relevance to the study of the organization of work. As sociologists have addressed issues of domination, control and class relations with respect to the organization of work, so they have returned to and developed the central concerns of Marx and Weber.

In the last chapter it was argued that for Weber bureaucracy was an imperatively co-ordinated system of control, which was fostered by capitalist rationality and the need for organizational calculability and discipline. Bureaucracy was, however, part of the general process of rationalization, and spread to all large-scale organizations, becoming a form of domination in itself. For Marx, large-scale organization of modern industry was also a form of despotic control, the direct result of attempts by capitalists to control and subordinate labour in their efforts to maximize profits.

There is clearly some common ground between Marx and Weber with respect to their analysis of the emergence and nature of modern work organizations. Both emphasized the existence of a class of formally free labour and of a free market in labour and the appropriation by employers of the ownership and control of the means of production. These conditions produced the separation of workers from ownership and control and their subordination and discipline at work and in the labour market. Both writers perceived that the despotic control exercised over workers was created by the pressure of competition and requirements for profitability. In both analyses, employers instigated rationalized methods of work organization and control, of which mechanization was a prime example, leading to the degradation and humiliation of the worker. The main difference between the two writers is, as several commentators have noticed,[1] that Marx's concept of alienation and the exploitative nature of the labour process is 'coupled with a sense of hope', whereas for Weber rationalization is a process which entails a fatalistic acceptance of the inevitability of the 'iron-cage'.

This chapter discusses, first, Marx's writing on the capitalist labour process and, second, the work of Braverman who brought the concept of the labour process centrally into the analysis of the contemporary organization of work. The last section of the chapter considers some of the main themes of the debate on the labour process which has continued since the publication of Braverman's book in the mid-1970s.[2]

MARX AND THE CAPITALIST LABOUR PROCESS

Marx's analysis of capitalism rests on a capital-labour relation in which a class of formally free wage earners are obliged to sell their labour power to earn their living, and a class of capitalists who, owning the physical means of production, purchase the labour power of workers, as a commodity, as another factor of production. However, in his mature work *Capital,* Vol I. Marx rests his analysis of the capital-labour relation on an abstract analysis of the capitalist mode of production as a system of commodity production and exchange. It is in this work that Marx develops an analysis of the capitalist labour process.

Marx's analysis of a commodity focuses on its dual character; it has both a use-value and an exchange-value. Use-values are products which serve to satisfy 'human needs of whatever kind' (1976, p.126). It is the usefulness of the thing, which is only realised in its use or in consumption. In a capitalist society, however, an employer not only has to produce a commodity which has a use-value, but one that has exchange-value in addition, that is, it is an article made to sell. A commodity has exchange-value when offered on an economic market in exchange for other products. Capitalist production is, therefore, production of goods which exchange in the market.

Marx argued that two commodities can be exchanged because they have one thing in common, that is, the amount of human labour that has been expended to create them. The value of any commodity depends, therefore, on the amount of labour embodied in it. More specifically, the value of a commodity is determined by the socially necessary labour time embodied in it. ('Socially necessary' meaning under certain average conditions of production given average skill and intensity of work prevalent at the time.)

Marx took over from the classical economists, Smith and Ricardo, the labour theory of value, in which the value of an object is measured by the amounts of labour time that went into its production. But Marx also held that labour is not only the measure of value, but its only source. Only living labour could create value; raw materials, machinery, and the physical means of production are dead labour. Only 'man's activity via the instruments of labour effects an alteration in the object of labour' (p.287).

It is not, however, labour that is sold to the capitalist but labour power—the capacity to work—which the employer has then to direct and supervise in the production process. Since labour power is bought and sold on the market it becomes a commodity which can be exchanged and its value determined. For Marx, the value of labour power was determined in the same way as any other commodity; as the amount of socially necessary time to reproduce it. That is, the wages a worker requires to enable himself and his family to subsist and reproduce in a condition fit to work.

But labour power is also a commodity unlike any other; it has the distinctive quality of not only creating value, but also of creating new value, a value greater than its own, namely surplus value. The process of creating surplus value, or the valorization process as Marx calls it, occurs because under certain conditions of production a worker can produce more than is necessary to cover the cost of his subsistence. If a worker works a ten-hour day, but only five hours is equivalent to his subsistence wage, then the employer has gained an excess of value through the surplus labour. Exploitation arises, therefore, because an employer has been able to extract from the worker more value than he is paid for a day's work. Such surplus value accrues to the employer as profits which, however, only become realised in the circulation of commodities. But the existence of surplus value is invisible, its origins concealed in a number of ways. Workers appear to receive wages for the entire day's work, profits are realised on the market and the size of profit appears to be determined by market forces of supply and demand.

In its simple and abstract element Marx sees the labour process as 'purposeful activity aimed at the production of use-values . . . an appropriation of what exists in nature for the requirements of man' (p.290). Under the capitalist process of production the aim is to produce exchange values which have a surplus value embodied in them. The labour process is at the same time, then, a valorization process. The labour process, 'when it is the process by which the capitalist consumes labour power' has two characteristics. First, the worker works under the control of the capitalist to whom his labour belongs, and secondly, 'the product is the property of the capitalist and not that of the worker, its immediate producer (p.292). Under the capitalist process of production labour power itself becomes a product or commodity belonging to the capitalist and 'the right to use that power for a day belongs to him, just as much as he has a right to use any other commodity . . .' (p.292).

That labour power is a commodity means that the worker functions as a thing, his labour power takes on the form of a commodity for himself, becoming objective and alien. Similarly 'the division of labour, use of the forces of labour and the sciences, the products of labour and machinery confront individual workers as alien, objective and ready made . . . independent of workers whom they dominate' (p.1054). The theme of alienated labour characteristic of Marx's early work, reappears in *Capital* but now as an activity which creates surplus value. The worker constantly produces material, objective wealth, but in the form of 'capital of an alien power that dominates and exploits him.'

Under the capitalist mode of production the transformation of all activities and products into commodities gives the appearance that the social world is characterized by relations between things, rather than by social relations between people. A process of reification, of the 'fetishism of commodities' take over in which people fail to understand the society which they have created. The capitalist system of commodity production appears as a natural order of contractual agreements between equals (capital and labour), and an equal exchange of wages for a fair day's work. Exploitation and the extraction of surplus value is hidden, for to all appearances the employer seems to pay for the whole day's work. But such reification is not, for Marx, a form of determinism, for the process of subordination and alienation of workers generates opposite and contradictory tendencies, leading to resistance and increasing class organization and class consciousness.

In *Capital,* Marx analyses the relentless drive for the accumulation and expansion of capital, for in competing with each other capitalists must maximize surplus value or go out of business. The compulsion to increase surplus value production implies a search for increased labour productivity. This can be achieved by prolonging the working day or, after the Factory Acts which restricted the length of the working day, by the intensification and mechanization of work. These latter methods, however, result in temporary competitive advantage since competitors catch up by adopting the same methods. Capital accumulation, therefore, involves the continual transformation of the organization and mechanization of the labour process. For this purpose Marx introduces a distinction between formal and real subordination of labour under capital. The movement from formal to real subordination involves a transformation in control of the labour process and the use of different methods in the extraction of surplus value.

The formal subordination of labour occurs at an early stage in the development of capitalism. Marx in fact, puts it from the mid-sixteenth century to the last third of the eighteenth century. In this early stage capitalists acquired the legal rights to finished products and to the realisation of profits through markets. Employers, however, had only formal domination of labour power for they often took over pre-existing methods of working in which workers themselves controlled their own work practices. In this phase of simple co-operation, in which previously independent craftsmen are brought together in one workshop, employers could realise only absolute surplus value by extending the length of the working day or by imposing a greater intensity and continuity of labour.

As Stark has said: 'For Marx the real subordination of labour occurred during the industrial revolution when capitalists transformed the organisational and technological basis of production' (1982, p.311). Marx analyses the real subordination of labour with respect to the second and third phases of capitalist production, namely, manufacture (the second phase), the increasingly complex co-operation and division of labour within the workplace, and modern large-scale industry (the third phase), brought about by the introduction of machinery, technology and science to the production process.

In the manufacturing phase the division of labour is extended, so that the work of 'detail labourers' is subdivided into the same type. The complex organization of the work of the resulting 'collective worker', that is, the joint activity of a number of detail workers, results in higher productivity, which increases relative surplus value. However, workers may still retain some control over their work practices because of their skills, 'customs and active resistance'.

Only in the third phase, modern large-scale industry, does labour become more completely subordinated to capital. Whilst the introduction of machinery, technology, and science to the production process increases relative surplus value by increasing the productivity of labour, it also cheapens and cripples the worker. It cheapens labour by reducing the labour time necessary for a worker to produce his subsistence. The more machinery is used the less living labour is available as a source of surplus value. The employer must therefore utilize the remaining labour power more effectively; his work is intensified, machinery speeded up or discipline tightened.

In the manufacturing phase the division of labour had crippled and fragmented the worker; in modern large-scale industry, machinery tortures and enslaves him, subjecting him to a 'despotism the more hateful for its meanness'. The worker becomes controlled by machinery 'out of which the power of the master is made'. There is a divorce of intellectual powers, that is experience, knowledge and skills, from the process of production, and the 'transformation of these powers into powers of capital over labour'. As a result workers become less skilled, require less training and are more easily replaceable. There is a 'tendency to equalize and reduce to an identical level every kind of work that has to be done by the minders of machines.'

The mechanization and transformation of the labour process creates a surplus population, an industrial reserve army, which can be used as cheap labour when required and expelled when not. As the simplified nature of jobs makes employed workers easily replaceable, the reserve army acts as a constant depression on wages and on worker resistance, intensifying still further the real subordination of labour. The immiseration thesis of Marx, 'that in portion as capital accumulates, the situation of the worker must grow worse', can be understood to involve an increase in the reserve army with its accumulation of misery and pauperism on the one hand, and the brutalization and moral degradation of the worker on the other.

BRAVERMAN

It is in the context of Marx's discussion of 'the labour process as it takes place under the control of capital' that Braverman in his book *Labour and Monopoly Capital* attempts to study 'the development of the capitalist mode of production over the past one hundred years' (p.4). The effect of the publication of Braverman's book in 1974 has been, as Sweezy suggested in the Foreword 'to pose rather than answer questions and to open (or reopen) lines of inquiry which have been neglected and which cry out for research and elaboration . . . In this sense [the] book is to be considered an invitation and a challenge . . .' (p.xii).

Braverman's study focuses on historical changes in the labour process and the structure of the American working class during this century. Following the distinction Marx made between the formal and real subordination of labour, Braverman suggests that the real subordination of labour occurred, not with the transition to large-scale industry, but rather at the turn of the twentieth century, with the application of Taylorism and scientific knowledge. Braverman argues that at the end of the nineteenth century the traditional knowledge and autonomy of the craftsmen still persisted, 'the workshops were run by the workers and not by the bosses' (p.102). Rather than an outmoded managerial ideology, Braverman shows that the achievement of Taylorism was the transformation of the labour process, in which the skills, knowledge and customs of the shop floor were displaced and 'embodied in a management [structure] dedicated to capitalist efficiency' (Stark 1982).

F.W. Taylor, an engineer and management consultant in late nineteenth-century America, believed that workers acting rationally in their own interests would, individually or collectively, restrict and control output. 'Scientific management' was Taylor's attempt to apply not only engineering principles to work processes but to systematize what he perceived as an incompetent management. Taylor set out to study methods and speeds of work, time taken, tools used, limb movements, fatigue, rest-pauses and other aspects of work organization, with a view to de-composing work tasks into a more efficient 'one best way' of production.

For Braverman, Taylor's 'scientific management' rested on three principles. First, management must systematically investigate and acquire knowledge and information about the ways in which work is carried out. Braverman calls this 'the dissociation of the labour process from the skills of the worker. The labour process is to be rendered independent of the craft, tradition and the workers' knowledge' (p.113). Secondly, the knowledge acquired by management is used for the purpose of planning work, thus removing 'all possible brain work from the shop floor' and 'concentrating it as an exclusive province of management' (p.113). Braverman calls this the principle of separation of conception from execution, preferring these terms to the more commonly used 'separation of mental from manual labour'. This is, he explains, because mental labour itself 'becomes subdivided rigorously according to the same rules'. The result of this principle was to fragment and standardize the division of labour so that individual workers were limited to the performance of single tasks, minimizing skill requirement and job-learning time. Lower-paid deskilled workers are then required, whose duty is to follow 'unthinkingly' 'simplified job tasks governed by simplified instructions' (p.118). Thirdly, management becomes responsible for planning, designing and monitoring the production process. Braverman calls this the 'use of this monopoly of knowledge to control each step of the labour process and its mode of execution'. Management is now able to determine, specify and monitor what tasks are to be done, how they are to be done and the exact time allowed for doing them. Labour control was thus built into the organization of work, into the fragmentation and routinization of the division of labour. Additional control was achieved by the use of incentive payments and bonus schemes fixed by Taylor's work study methods.

Although Taylorism was for Braverman the prime method of managerial control over labour, he also sees mechanization as a mode of control in which workers' skills and knowledge are increasingly incorporated into machines. The effect in both cases is the degradation and deskilling of work, as technical and scientific knowledge of working craftsmanship is destroyed. This is so, too, for office workers, and service and retail workers who similarly experience rigorous control, increased division of labour, mechanization and simplification of tasks.

Braverman suggests that 'two-thirds to three-fourths of the working population appears readily to conform to the dispossessed condition of a proletariat', 'a giant mass of workers who are relatively homogeneous as to lack of developed skill, low pay and interchangeability of person and function' (p.35). He further implies that the 'middle layers' of employment, the lower ranks of supervision and management, specialized and professional employees occupied in marketing, finance and administration, as well as hospitals, schools, and government administration, will find themselves similarly subject to forms of work rationalization and proletarianization. In their class position, however, such 'middle-level' workers share the characteristics of both workers and managers, in that they both sell their labour power and in varying degrees are engaged in controlling the labour of others.

Braverman's discussion of welfare work is rather general and tangential to his discussion of the expansion of the service sector. The creation of a 'universal market' involves the commodification of all those spheres of life previously outside market relations, for example, food production, recreation and social services. In this process the caring and welfare services formally provided in the family and the community are now produced in a commodity form, particularly by women who now work as degraded labour in the non-unionized, low-waged service sector. Additionally, there is an expansion of the state's services to ameliorate 'poverty and insecurity' and the embittered and antagonistic social life of the cities which 'threaten the very existence of the social structure'.

In a separate chapter Braverman addresses himself to Marx's distinction between productive and unproductive labour. However, he finds this is no longer a useful distinction to make as all labour, whether it produces, realises or diverts surplus labour, is organized along lines laid down in the productive sector and 'labour becomes an undifferentiated mass'.

The major theme of Braverman's work is thus that the transformation of the labour process results in degradation and deskilling of the working class. He presents a view of 'a class whose members have progressively become receptacles of abstract labour, de-skilled and de-cultured, atomized, monitored and measured to one thousandth of a second at work, and manipulated into consuming useless commodities at home' (Coombs 1978, p.93). This pessimistic view stems partly from his self-imposed limitation of an intention to study the 'objective' side of class, 'the class in itself', not the 'consciousness, organisation and activities' of the modern working class. As we shall see, this has led several commentators to observe that, for Braverman, classes are characterized solely by their economic positions and not in terms of relations that involve the conscious activity of human agents.

THE POST-BRAVERMAN DEBATE

The stimulus to the debate following the publication of Braverman's book was provided by several weaknesses in Braverman's work. Most important amongst the criticisms levelled at Braverman is his portrayal of management as conspiratorial and omniscient, dominating a passive and unresistant workforce. Both employers and workers are seen in functionalist terms as acting out and complying with the requirements of capital accumulation. Consequently, there is no allowance in his scheme for the ways in which active resistance and struggles on the part of workers have themselves shaped both the labour process and managements' subsequent responses. 'The essence of the mistake made by Braverman is to imply that the domination of labour by capital within the labour process is virtually complete' (Coombs 1978, p.94).

Other writers have drawn attention to the pessimism of Braverman and its similarities to that of Weber. Each, for example, perceived 'a one way movement of power away from those at the lower levels of the organization (Giddens 1982, p.93). In this respect Stark has remarked that Braverman's work 'begins with Marx's theory of value but ends with Weber's iron cage' (1982, p.314).[3]

Further criticisms of Braverman have concerned his concentration on Taylorism as the most important management strategy and his assumption of a universal adoption and implementation of Taylorism. He has been accused of romanticizing and idealizing craft work and of presenting an inexorable progression towards the deskilling of jobs. Finally the centrality of control over the labour process in relation to capital concentration and accumulation has been questioned, for investment strategies and product market decisions may be as important.

Yet despite these criticisms there is general agreement that Braverman raised important questions which have led to a renewed interest in the organization and control of the labour process. Whilst some have seen this interest as an affliction of Bravermania (for example Littler and Salaman 1982) there is no doubt 'that industrial sociology, industrial relations and organization theory were all changed and redirected by Braverman's book' (Burrell 1986). As a consequence there has been a wide debate on the reorganization of the labour process in the twentieth century, focusing on, for example, variations in managerial control strategies, the effects of worker resistance and processes of deskilling and reskilling. Some of the main themes of this debate are discussed below, in particular the problematic concepts of control and management strategy.

The Concept of Control
One important area of debate has concerned Braverman's neglect of forms of worker resistance to managerial control strategies. A number of studies have now shown that historically and cross-nationally there have been wide variations in the ability of organized labour to resist or influence managerial controls (Littler 1982, Gospel and Littler 1983, and see Chapter 6 on the USA and UK). Theoretically too, attention has focused on what has been called the subjective dimension in the labour process, the variability of labour power or the 'central indeterminacy of labour potential' as Littler has termed it (1982, p.31). Mention has already been made of criticisms of Braverman's emphasis on the structural transformation of work, his self-imposed limitation to the objective content of class and his neglect of the subjective, conscious dimension of labour activity. In contrast to this, many recent writers on the labour process have called for a dialectical analysis which takes into account both structure and agency within the labour process (Edwards 1983c, Willmott 1985, Storey 1985). These writers argue that there is a dynamic interplay between control and resistance so that control processes are understood as emergent processes continually shaped by the interaction between management and employee intentions and responses.

The Frontier of Control

In this context the term 'frontier of control' has been used to suggest the way in which the balance of power between management and workers can shift. Stark for example has remarked that 'minor skirmishes over the pace of work, the persistence of informal work groups which attempt to regulate output, the organized struggle over the hours, conditions and supervision of work [are] important ways in which the labour process is a "frontier of control" the scope and depth of which is determined by the degree of militancy and the forms of organization of the working class' (1982, p.314).

The notion of the frontier of control suggests then that work practices become a shifting arena of struggles between contending groups and that those groups subordinate in the hierarchy are not always the losers. In Braverman's treatment for instance it has been pointed out that he viewed the labour process as a zero sum concept in which managers acquire control or knowledge in a once and for all process; workers are deemed to have lost control and are not able to regain it. However, increased management control as for instance in the introduction of work study and incentive bonus schemes, may simultaneously increase the basis of worker organization and resistance and hence control (Rubery 1978, Wood and Kelly 1982).

The concept of a frontier of control has been taken further by introducing Strauss's notion of 'negotiated order' (1963; see also Chapter 1). The frontier of control is then seen as fluid and shifting, continually changing on a day-to-day basis (Littler 1982). The immediate or local control of work practices is the result of strategies of bargaining and conflicts between the contending hierarchical and occupational groups. Particular working arrangements may then emerge through trade-offs, compromises, the making of deals, collusion and the other subprocesses documented by Strauss (1978). Such a negotiated order involves a learning process in which management and the different occupational and work groups learn from and accommodate to the others' past behaviour.

Forms of control

The changing frontier of control and ability of workers to

resist is, however, limited by the totality of the structural relation between capital and labour. Here the distinction made by Edwards (1983c) between general control and immediate control is useful; general control refers to the form of organization of work which ensures the continuing securing of surplus value; immediate control refers to the ability to direct the details of work operations themselves (a similar point is also made by Friedman 1977). Whilst there is an imperative to general control, the form this takes at an empirical level is open to the choices and actions of the participants involved.

Several writers have emphasized that in contrast to Braverman's unidimensional approach of Taylorism and deskilling there are a variety of means of management control which do not always involve the deskilling of workers. Writers have acknowledged that Taylorism has been important in some circumstances but that other modes of control may be more important in other conditions. Hence a variety of control methods have been indentified which have been applied in different phases of capitalism (Edwards 1979, Burawoy 1979), to different groups of workers (Friedman 1977), and in different countries (Littler 1982). The works of Friedman and Edwards are now classic studies of the labour process as both attempted to include forms of worker resistance in their analysis and to substitute other means of management control for that of Taylorism and deskilling.

Edwards, in his book *Contested Terrain,* has documented 'the way in which capitalists have attempted to organize production in such a way as to minimize workers' opportunities for resistance'. Historically, he argues, there have been three different management strategies of control, each strategy emerging as a result of past conflicts and struggles between workers and employes. The first system of control he terms 'simple control' in which employers exercise power openly, arbitrarily, and personally. Simple control formed the organizational basis of nineteenth-century firms and continues today in small enterprises of the most competitive industries. The second form of control is technical, the control mechanism embedded in the physical technology of the firm, the third is bureaucratic control which is located in the social organization of the enterprise. These last two systems of control constitute 'structural forms of control, in the sense that the exercise of power becomes institutionalized in the very structure of the firm and is thus made impersonal' (1981, p.161).

Edwards considers the bureaucratic mode to be a major capitalist control strategy for power relations become invisible, embedded in impersonal rules and procedures. Moreover, segmented labour markets arise from the way in which the labour process is controlled, hence the bureaucratic mode of control gives rise to internal labour markets in which various mechanisms such as career ladders, salary rises, job security and fringe benefits are used to tie the worker to the organization.

Edwards' work has however been considered to be flawed in a number of respects, in particular in its over-emphasis of uniliniar management strategies and its underestimate of worker resistance. Some writers have argued that segmented labour markets are not just the product of employers' strategies, but that defensive tactics by organized groups of workers have also been important in shaping the structure of labour markets, divisions of labour and associated levels of pay and rewards (Friedman 1977, Kreckel 1980, and Rubery 1978; see also Chapters 4 and 5).[4]

Friedman in his book *Industry and Labour* has contended that as a result of resistance and accommodation within the labour process management have devised an alternative and less coercive technique of control. In addition to forms of direct control such as Taylorism, a form of control which Friedman describes as 'responsible autonomy' has been used by management to harness the creative potential of workers. Responsible autonomy is characterized by management attempts to win the loyalty and co-operation of workers by giving them greater work autonomy, increased income or better conditions of work, or by introducing participation, job enrichment or job enlargement schemes. Friedman suggests that responsible autonomy is more applicable to centrally placed, relatively privileged and skilled workers, whilst direct control is more likely to be used for peripheral workers whose labour is not crucial to the overall operation of the firm. Peripheral workers tend to be weakly organized, have little responsibility and are subject to close supervision.

Friedman's analysis directs attention to ways in which certain groups of workers within an organization are vulnerable to direct control while some are not, although it is not clear from his scheme to what extent management has given some workers responsible autonomy as concessions or the work groups themselves have achieved these privileges through the use of successful strategies of control or exclusion directed at other occupational groups. This is a question to which we return in Chapters 4 and 5 in discussions of the privileged labour market position of professionals and other highly-educated workers.

These earlier studies of different types of management control assumed that when particular forms of control failed new control structures were devised which solved the problem and ensured continued accumulation of surplus value. Workers were then said to have lost control over their craft skills and control over production. Littler refers to the search for one control strategy which provides a total solution as the 'panacea fallacy' (1982). Storey (1985) in contrast has argued that the evidence of empirical studies suggests rather that the means of management control are complex and diverse and can be applied simultaneously at different levels within the organization, both vertically and alongside each other. For example new technology, financial controls, labour restructuring, and new welfare styles may all be applied simultaneously, although there may be different degrees of connectedness between them. An important point here is that control systems are indeterminate, they do not rest on a 'single precarious control mode' which once introduced means that labour's challenge to management disappears, but on multiple controls which have to be continuously reconstituted in the face of a continual contestation by labour.

Control structures are also indeterminate because they contain, as Storey puts it, 'their own inherent contradictions [which] undermine any ultimate or absolute logic in the means of control' (1985, p.197). Employers may impose control structures which involve workers in a 'relation of minimum interaction' (Littler 1982) but they are still dependent on the subjective dimension of the production process, the worker's control of his or her own labour power. The imposition of managerial control systems which rationalize away the subjective dimension of work, such as claims to pride, or moral commitment, stand in danger of being self-defeating, generating further problems and tensions for management which it then has to resolve. It is for this reason, as we discuss below, that management has also had to devise strategies which elicit the co-operation and compliance of workers.

Contradictions can appear at other levels too. For example, as we discuss in Chapters 3 and 8, attempts by state managers to impose new methods of management control on state welfare organizations, especially those derived from the private sector, tend to undermine the purposes of organizations orientated to social welfare criteria. Managers then become subject to a diffuse set of political pressures, as subordinate and opposition groups can use the multiple social welfare aims of public welfare services to deny the validity of management claims and policies.

The Problem of Control
The need for the control of labour power arose, Marx believed, because labour power is a commodity unlike any other commodity. He called labour power 'variable capital' indicating that it is controlled by an independent will. Then as now the problem for employers is to direct this autonomous and unknown potential to the employer's own ends.

The problem of control is not however confined to the workplace; schools, family, religion and class subcultures are also engaged in the preparation of attitudes to and expectations of work and authority. Employees come to work with a variety of orientations ranging from deference, passive acquiescence, and instrumental compliance to moral commitment. In Chapter 5, for example, we argue that one of the reasons why higher-educated and professional workers obtain positions of trust and delegated authority within organizations is because their professional or educational socialization prior to entry into the organization may produce work attitudes which are conducive to the goals of the organization.

The indeterminancy or variability of labour power, described by Friedman as 'a potentially malleable commodity', has received attention from writers who have stressed the need for employers to harness the creativity and co-operation of labour power. Friedman, as we have seen, argued that the potential for workers to resist or be non-co-operative meant that employers had to devise less coercive means of control which elicit the creative potential of labour power. Cressey and McInnes also note that employers must 'in practice . . . surrender the means of production to the "control" of workers for their actual *use* in the production process', hence they must 'to some degree seek a cooperative relation with [workers]' (1980, p14).

Burawoy (1979) has argued that Marx's analysis of the labour process rested on the assumption that the expenditure of effort is decided by coercion. Marx had no place in his theory of the labour process for the organization of consent, for the necessity to elicit a willingness to co-operate in the translation of labour power into labour. As Burawoy notes, this is not surprising given the despotic conditions of work during the nineteenth century. In the twentieth century, he argues (1985), state intervention has broken the economic whip of nineteenth-century employers by introducing social insurance that guarantees the reproduction of labour power independently of participation in the workplace, and by circumscribing the methods of managerial domination through labour legislation, trade union recognition and collective bargaining procedures. (The different forms of state intervention both in the reproduction of labour power and in workplace relations are considered with reference to the USA and the UK in Chapter 6). Now workers must be persuaded to co-operate with management, and the labour process has to be understood as 'the result of different combinations of force and consent'.

Management

Braverman defines management as 'a complex of staff organizations suited to a subdivision of authority by various specialized functions' (1974, p.267). But these various specialist groups together still perform the corporate function of the control of capital organization and its workforce. Braverman's suggestion that management is now 'a labour process for the purpose of control . . . and is conducted as a labour process exactly analogous to the process of production' (p.267) is important for he implies that the same processes of fragmentation and routinization are occurring in the management process itself.

However, the link which Braverman drew between the imperative of capital accumulation and managerial control structures has more recently been regarded as too problematic. It has been argued that management is not 'omniscient, monolithic and homogeneous', but rather is internally differentiated itself into sectional groups with their own interests, identities and objectives (Wood and Kelly 1982, Salaman 1982). Drawing on pluralist perspectives these authors suggest that managerial policies will be the outcome of processes of internal bargaining and conflicts between these sectional groups. Policies that derive from these conflicts then require to be translated into specific operational practices to achieve them, but as Wardell (1986) notes, once managerial decisions are known they then become the basis on which groups lower down the hierarchy organize their resistance and responses. Management not only has to cope with the tensions that such resistance generates but must also work at the continual reassertion of control.

The concept of management strategy has also received considerable attention in the labour process and industrial relations literature, since a number of doubts have been raised as to the usefulness of the concept. First, several writers have argued that the concept of strategy implies consciously planned and long-term policies, which may impute a rationality or coherence to managerial intentions which do not exist. As we have seen in Chapter 1 the rationality of managerial actions and the relationship of organizational goals to structures is problematic. In the labour process literature doubts about the coherence and rationality of managerial strategy have been expressed most forcefully by Rose and Jones (1985). On the basis of their research into six industrial organizations they suggest that management policy making and execution is 'piecemeal, uncoordinated and empiricist' (1985, p.99).

Second, other writers have questioned the extent to which management policy may not always have the conscious

intention of controlling labour, as product markets or investment decisions may be more important at different times.
Salaman and Littler point out that 'capitalists are not after all
. . . interested in control per se. The first priority is accumulation not control. Accumulation may at times be better
served by investment, accounting, product or marketing
policies rather than labour control' (1984, p.64). In Chapter 7
it is also argued that in the state welfare sector as well as
policies directed to the control of labour affairs, government
policies have to be implemented which embody welfare
criteria directed to social needs and principles of equity.

Third, Wood and Kelly (1982) have argued that the existence of managerial policies should not be taken as evidence
of their implementation, for policies can be reinterpreted and
poorly understood by lower-level managers, can have unintended consequences, and as we argued in the previous
section can be resisted and subverted by groups at all levels in
the organization.

Although many of these criticisms of the concept of managerial strategy are valid, the limitations surrounding the
concept can be accommodated so that the concept remains a
useful one (Child 1985, Storey 1985, Thurley and Wood
1982). With respect to the first criticism Child observes that
although management strategies may be unspecific and
incoherent they may nevertheless have relevance for the
labour process. 'In capitalist economies corporate management strategies will necessarily reflect a consciousness of
certain general objectives which are the normal conditions for
organizational survival' (1985, p.110). These objectives may
not be a conscious 'strategic campaign plan' but, as Storey
has also suggested, a structure and style pattern may be
devised which strive towards a set of initiatives that fall
between a grand strategy and muddling through (1985,
p.202).

On the second criticism Child has remarked that although
management policies may not be taken with reference to the
control of labour they nonetheless may have implications for
the labour process and the conditions and terms of employment of employees (1985, p.111). This point is picked up in
Chapter 7 with reference to changes in the conditions of terms

of work of state welfare employees. Lastly the 'degree to which management holds and operates a strategy' and the extent to which that strategy is actually implemented has to be, as Wood and Kelly note, empirically determined, as do the processes which intervene in that implementation.

CONCLUSION

Labour process analysis provides an important framework for the study of the capitalist organization of work, as it links specific management policies to wider issues of power and class relations. Despite major criticisms the approach remains influential, as Braverman's work has been supplemented by insights derived from the sociology of organizations and work. As we have seen, recent studies have developed more historically and empirically informed accounts of management practices by documenting the ways in which different structures and types of control have varied by plant, industry, over time and cross-nationally. Yet more recently it has been argued that the range of criticisms based on the details of empirical studies (as Burrell [1986] notes in line with the British tradition of empiricism, falsification and counter-factuals) is in danger of losing sight of the core theory of the labour process. This is Thompson's thesis in a recent paper entitled 'Crawling from the Wreckage' in which he reviews criticisms of labour process theory. He points out that 'Without such a framework [that is the core theory] there is a danger of returning to an empiricist tradition of accumulating plant studies, differentiated only by appropriating the language some seem so keen to discard' (1986, p.1).

There remain however problems of the limitations of labour process analysis, for example, little regard has been paid to the complexities of contemporary work outside the employment of male workers in manufacturing industries. Consequently the implications of the employment of large numbers of workers in state welfare organizations, of the development of gendered and ethnic divisions of labour and of the increased significance of large numbers of highly educated workers have received little attention from within the mainstream labour process literature. These areas are discussed in Chapters 3, 4 and 5 respectively where we note that contributions have come from those outside the labour process tradition, from critical theorists, from feminist writers and from the sociology of the professions.

NOTES

1. For example Loewith (1970), and Turner (1981).
2. For a discussion of why a concern with Marx's analysis of the labour process was neglected until the publication of Braverman's book see Braverman pp.9-13, and Thompson (1983).
3. Littler (1982) however has made an important distinction between the Weberian model and Taylorism as described by Braverman. 'Taylorism represents the bureaucratization of the structure of control not the employment relationship'. There is in Taylorism no career structure, instead it involves what Littler calls the 'minimum interaction relation', that is, Taylorism produces easy substitutability of workers in terms of skill and training, reducing the organization's dependence on the availability, ability and motivation of individuals. The Weberian model on the other hand incorporates the notion of career, promotion and appointment on the basis of expertise and professional qualifications.
4. Batstone *et al.* in an important critique suggest that 'Edwards' concept of bureaucratic control is incapable of capturing the complexities of the labour control strategies to which it refers' (1984, p.290). The authors point out that Edwards' account underplays the extent to which segmentation of the labour force, by introducing inflexibility, sectional divisions and grade rivalries, can in fact be costly for management rather than advantageous and, second, Edwards ignores the way in which bureaucratic rules may be manipulated by those supposedly controlled by them, thus undermining the effectiveness of bureaucratic control. Third, Edwards does not distinguish between rules that are unilaterally imposed by management and those that are jointly determined by management and unions, and fourth, Edwards does not consider the contradictions engendered by management, strategies, particularly the ways in which control structures can damage the commitment of the workforce. Lastly the authors point out that Edwards does not theorize the way in which different strategies may be adopted towards different groups within the same organization.

3 The Labour Process in the State Welfare Sector

As the discussion in the last chapter has shown, the labour process debate has paid scant attention to the growth and importance of the state as employer in the post-war period. Consequently, there has, from this perspective, been little written on the management of state agencies and changes which have occurred in the organization and control of state work.

The theme of this chapter is to point to structural properties of state modes of organization which may differentiate them from capitalist organizations and condition worker and management strategies. This analysis is located within a framework which considers that although labour processes in state and private sectors are similar, each is governed by a different criterion of rationality. In this regard, the analytic distinctions drawn by Offe (1976) in conjunction with Habermas (1976) and O'Connor (1973) between the different modes of rationality governing state and private sectors, are discussed.

An analysis of state labour processes should include consideration of the relation of state production of goods and services to both the capital accumulation process and the democratic processes. It is in relation to both accumulation and legitimation that the state's activities have become the source of new contradictions and political divisions in the 1970s and 1980s. Such an analysis should also, as Fryer (1983) has argued, take into account the rapid growth of state employment, trade unionism and the rationalizations and reorganizations of work which have incorporated Taylorist and other principles of labour control.

Empirical evidence on the management of the state's labour force is to be found in the more conventional academic disciplines such as organizational analysis, and public administration. A number of such studies, however, have been concerned with prescribing the most 'rational' or 'efficient' mode of organizing and managing state agencies, and have themselves been influential in the design of 'appropriate' management structures and the hierarchic forms which were imposed on state welfare organizations in the 1970s.[1] Other writers, though, have rejected this 'managerial' model and, influenced by perspectives developed in organization sociology, have focused instead on a model of the organization as a plurality of competing groups and coalitions. Organizational structure and policies are then perceived as the outcome of a political process from which a dominant coalition emerges and succeeds in imposing its preferences and values on the organization. (Child 1972, Hunter 1979, Haywood and Alaszewski 1980, Ham 1981.)

A view of the organization as a political, negotiated process has been of especial value in drawing attention to the different ideologies and sources of power actors bring to their work situation and to the policy-making process, and to the ways in which different groups can influence or resist managerial choices. Such studies have also shown that formal management arrangements often have a limited influence on work processes. Burns, in a perceptive study of NHS hospitals, found that much of the work was accomplished by a collaborative system[2] which was not 'subject to, or the consequence of, sets of instructions and specific routines laid down by management' (1981, p.4). Other studies have found that the 'power of managers in the NHS to effect change is very limited' (Haywood and Alaszewski 1980, p.149), since the medical profession is able to define the purpose of the health services and control the actual delivery and general development of services (cf. also Hunter 1979, and Ham 1981). However although these approaches are empirically valuable and are sensitive to the complexities of management in organizations which contain groups with quite different rationales, there is a tendency to neutralize the environment of the state's activities and to ignore the structural constraints implicit in the state's role in a capitalist economy.

In the labour process literature, on the other hand, the link which Braverman has drawn between the imperatives of capitalist accumulation and managerial control structures has recently been regarded as too 'automatic, unmediated and unproblematic (Salaman, 1982). Wood and Kelly (1982) and Salaman (1982) argue, for example, that management is not, as Braverman implies, homogeneous, omniscient and con-spiratorial, but that the internal differentiation of management generates sectional groups with their own interests, identities and objectives. Drawing on pluralist studies these authors suggest that processes of internal bargaining and conflict between these groups will mediate between system requirements and the labour process as Braverman describes it. Other writers have developed more historically and empirically informed accounts of manage-ment practices by documenting the ways in which different structures and types of managerial control have varied by plant, industry, overtime and cross-nationally. (Littler 1982, Gospel and Littler 1983, Friedman 1977.) But almost all of these studies concern themselves with the private manu-facturing sector of the economy and few have considered the different economic and organizational context of state management.

There are exceptions though. For example one treatment of 'non-capitalist state activities' is to be found in those discussions of the class location and work situations of state service workers as unproductive workers. (Carchedi 1977, Crompton and Gubbay 1977, and Crompton and Jones, 1984.) In these schemes, state employees are regarded as being as oppressed as employees in privately-owned enter-prises (even though the latter produce surplus value and the former do not), since the work of both is controlled and supervised by management. Both state and private sector workers are subsumed under the authority of employers by virtue of the fact that they sell their labour power and surrender the creative capacity of their labour. Crompton and Jones note that although it may be theoretically incorrect to describe state service managers as capitalists, 'they are nevertheless constrained to act as "capitalists" in respect of the organization and control of their labour force' (1984, p.214). Although this analysis seemingly makes the concept of surplus value redundant, it is correct in pointing to similarities in the labour processes of state and private sector workers. In the post-war period forms of capitalist rationality have been introduced into state organizations and state managers are required to act, as do those in the private sector, according to principles of cost-efficiency and productivity in order to contain costs. But, as is argued later in this chapter, state managers are not just constrained to 'act as capitalists' but are also subject to a non-market rationality which does have consequences for state managers and workers.

A further view of state management is to be found in the now considerable literature, from a Marxist or neo-Marxist perspective, on the role of the state under conditions of advanced capitalism. These discussions are mainly theoretical in treatment, and in social welfare provision have focused on the structural constraints that shape state intervention. Writers such as O'Connor (1973), Gough (1979) and the CSE State Group (1979) have presented careful analyses of the contradictions generated by the development of the state's welfare activities. In this respect Gough has argued that whilst the Keynesian welfare state helped sustain the economic and social relations of capitalism, it generated contradictory tendencies, namely, 'the exacerbation of class conflict over the distribution of the national product, and the undermining of the production of the surplus product' (1983, p.472). In turn, these contradictions have given rise to the restructuring of the welfare state which is explained by Gough as the 'state acting in the long-term interests of capital.' (1979, p.141).[3] Gough recognizes however that re-structuring is restricted by the prior and existing organizations of the welfare state and by the interests of the professionals, trade unions and clients' movements thus affected.

The CSE State Group also attempts to show that 'management structures within the state apparatus have been developed in order to maintain long-term ideological domination and effective day to day control, so that the long-term interests of capital in general are furthered,' (1979, p.122). They note, however, that 'the state has no magic way of knowing what is in the interests of capital.' 'For there is a certain arbitrariness in the rules and norms that guide the management of state agencies. Unlike the private sector they are not subject to the law of value.' (pp.21-2).

The view that state managers simply act in accord with the interests of a 'far-sighted capitalist class or as the automatic functional response of the political system to the needs of capitalism' has been challenged by Theda Skocpol (1980, p.200). In her study of the US New Deal she agrees that neo-Marxist analyses are more promising than others in explaining political conflict and transformation within advanced capitalism, but she considers that 'state organizations have their own structures, their own histories and their own patterns of conflict and impact upon class relations and economic development' (1980, p.200). In other words state management is embedded in a political apparatus with its own mode of rationality.

The different organizational logics or modes of rationality governing state and private sectors have been recognized by writers such as O'Connor (1973), Habermas (1976) and Offe (1976). In privately owned enterprises management acts in ways which serve and legitimize the form of property for which they work, i.e. they are governed by the logic of maximizing profits. Habermas notes, for example, that in the private sector there are clear and finite parameters which surround capital and labour relations, the social consequences of which are bankruptcy and unemployment. In the state welfare sector this logic does not apply. The provision of services is governed by non-market criteria and parameters, for example, public policy making and budgetary decisions. Policy formation, however, takes place in the context of a diffusion of objectives between political concerns, interest-group demands, professional and other provider groups as well as budgetary constraints. Consequently there are no clear criteria that can be applied in the assessment of efficiency or effectiveness, as the state's activities 'cannot be calculated in monetary terms, since they are not sold on a market' (Offe 1975b, p.139). Rather, the thresholds or parameters of the state's activities are those of legitimation: 'irrational or inefficient decisions by state administrators may result in social disorganization or deprivation but these consequences are not strictly quantifiable . . . it depends on the population as to what are regarded as tolerable disruptions to social life' (Frankel 1982, p.271).

Because of discrepancies in rationality between state and private sector organizations, Habermas and Offe contend that the state cannot act as a 'class-conscious political organ' which is able to plan self-consciously and effectively for the reproduction of capital. Rather, because the state has to operate according to its own administrative logic and cannot directly control private investment or production, it has a deficient planning capacity, characterized by a vacillation of policies, a 'muddling through' and a 'reactive avoidance of crisis.'

By differentiating between labour processes in private and state sector organizations Habermas, Offe and O'Connor are able to distinguish different relations of production in each social formation. The theoretical difficulties which surround discussion of state workers in labour process theory (although not in Braverman's work) namely, that state workers are unproductive workers who do not produce surplus value, are overcome in the writings of these theorists. For as Frankel (1982) remarks, critical theorists move beyond the debate about productive or unproductive labour to consider state labour as not only reproducing capitalist social relations but also as negating them.

Habermas and Offe claim that advanced capitalism cannot be understood solely in terms of exchange relations of capital and wage-labour, but that productive state activity itself brings into being new and additional forms of social relations of production. Yet, although the commodity form depends upon the extension of these productive state activities, the latter nevertheless tend to undermine the dominance of the capital relation, and thus the conditions on which their survival depends. Not only do productive state activities exacerbate the fiscal crisis of governments, but the state itself can become the possible focus of political and social conflict over the way in which societal resources should be utilized.

It would seem then that critical theorists have important insights to offer on the 'contradictory role which present states have to sustain' (Frankel, 1982) which includes their role as employer. In addition, Offe has been one of the few writers to provide a theory of the capitalist state which also considers its internal mode of operation. The following discussion is therefore an attempt to relate the theoretical propositions of the critical theorists to the organization and control of state welfare work.

The following discussion is divided into two parts: the first examines the links which Offe has drawn between a theory of the capitalist state, public policy making and the state's internal mode of organization. Developing the view that the state has a limited capacity for rational administration, Offe argues that the state's key problem is how to 'devise' modes of internal organization which will be 'adequate' to meet pressures both from the requirement to sustain the accumulation process and from certain non-capitalist interests represented through the political process. Moreover, Offe spells out the mechanisms by which the administrative activities of the state do not necessarily always guarantee that the interests of capital will be secured, as the state is also dependent on the compliance of organized professional and labour elites. The implications of these propositions are considered in later chapters: first, for the structuring of work and divisions of labour amongst the welfare provider groups (Chapter 5) and second, in state managers' attempts to impose appropriate forms of organization on state welfare work (Chapters 7 and 8).

The second section examines Offe's analysis of the structurally contradictory position of the state's welfare activities, government attempts to resolve these contradictions and lastly (and the most criticized aspect of his thesis) the limits to state policy making. These arguments are related to the current restructuring of state welfare work in Chapters 7 and 8. The arguments of Habermas, Offe and O'Connor are also discussed in Chapter 6 in relation to the different spheres of production in the private and state sectors, the fiscal crisis of the USA and UK states in the 1970s and the implications for public sector trade unions, workers and clients.

INTERNAL ORGANIZATION OF THE STATE AND POLICY FORMATION

Offe distinguishes different modes of state intervention as allocative and productive state activities. In allocative activities the state possesses the authority to allocate resources acquired from taxation, for example, social security payments or protective tariffs to industry. Under conditions of advanced capitalism, however, allocative policies have to be augmented by productive activities which individual capitals are incapable of creating, finding them too risky or costly. Productive activities such as the health, education and social services, and research and development require some physical input in the nature of raw materials, capital investment and labour (1975a).

For Offe, explanations of social policy must take into account both 'demands' from the 'political processing of class conflict' and 'system requirements' of the accumulation process. The key problem for social policy formation, however, is the extent to which modes of internal organization of the state apparatus can be devised which make compatible these two poles of the 'needs' of capital and labour (1984).

Offe (1975a) suggests that the state's allocative and productive activities are capable of being organized in accordance with three modes of operation.

Firstly, the bureaucratic mode, which arises when state resources are allocated in a routine way, applying predetermined rules through hierarchical structures.

Secondly, the purposive-rational mode, planning inspired by technical rationality, such as cost-benefit analysis, performance indicators and control by objectives.

Thirdly, the democratic mode of political conflict and consensus.

Offe argues that none of these three logics of policy production provides an adequate structural basis for the state to reconcile its contradictory pressures of accumulation and legitimation. Bureaucratic modes, although suited to allocative state activities, are too routinized, rigid and ineffective for the state's productive activities. This is intended as a critique of the Weberian thesis; namely 'the superior efficiency of bureaucratic structures', which in Offe's view is only of limited relevance to the organization of many state activities.

In the second mode, however, the criteria of rationality governing state organizations create a number of obstacles to the application of purposive rationality. Such techniques are similar to those in industrial commodity production, but whereas private industry has clear criteria of effectiveness and efficiency, the state does not possess 'unequivocal, uncontroversial or operational cues as to what the goals of its productive activities should be'. In addition, the resources required for long-term planning attempts interfere with the prerogatives of the accumulation process, or conversely, the well-known problem of state welfare programmes being blocked by limitations on state spending.

Lastly, the democratic process of political conflict/consensus, as a mode of organization, can lead to unlimited demands by working-class and non-capitalist interests which became subversive of the balance between the state and the accumulation process. At the level of local government this is a useful argument for, as Saunders has shown, the state is here relatively responsive to popular demands (1983). It is for the reasons suggested by Offe that the dynamic of state production has 'shifted through increasing concentration and scale, to the regional and central levels of the system' (Cawson and Saunders 1983).

The inadequacy of these three modes of operation implies that it is difficult for the state to devise forms of internal organization which make compatible political demands and the requirements of capital accumulation. Hence the vacillation of governments between a number of strategies in the management of state services, reorganizations, efficiency drives, privatization, and centralization.

The 'structural selectivity' of the state, however, means that there is no guarantee that these internal modes of organization will either secure or serve the interests of capital or the interests and needs of unorganized and marginal groups. In a variant of corporatist theory, Offe suggests elsewhere (1972) that those groups representing institutionalized interests, fractions of capital, organized labour and professional elites, who are able to make the most effective contribution to the avoidance of risks, are granted 'structurally determined privileges'. The state selectively intervenes, so that these groups are able to define the scope of 'realistic' issues and demands, which are then filtered through political and administrative processes. As a consequence, general social interests which are not institutionally organized, and peripheral groups and depressed areas which do not generate dangers to the system, are excluded from access to political decision-making. Moreover, a new technocratic concept of politics becomes relevant where public policy making is not directed to the solution of 'correct and just vital reforms', but to the 'conservation of social relations which claim mere functionality as their justification'. Offe points here to the repressive character of the state, in which the articulation of a wide range of democractic interests and needs is excluded and depoliticized.

As Cawson (1982) has noted, Offe's analysis of allocative and productive state activities and their organizational forms is of value in explaining the differences in political process in various social policy areas. For example, whilst allocative policy is most effectively administered through a bureaucratic organization, 'the production of welfare services involves the collaboration of professional providers in the determination of goals' (Cawson 1982). The production of welfare services is 'adequate' not because it conforms to pre-determined rules and procedures, as in allocative activities, but because it leads to certain results or policy goals.

But as we have seen there is no simple relationship between goals, organizational activity and final outcomes or quality of welfare services. Moreover, clients themselves do not, as do customer preferences in the private market, create demands, for these are largely defined and controlled by the professional providers. Lacking clear criteria of their own, state administrators have, therefore, depended on the professional providers' judgement as to what are adequate resources and types of treatment. This has meant not only that the professional provider groups have had an expansionary impact on state welfare budgets, but also that the interests of the more powerful professions have been privileged. This mutual compliance and dependence between the state and the professional provider groups has been important in the structuring of work and divisions of labour, as well as in the determination of social policies. (These arguments are discussed more fully in Chapter 5).

THE LIMITS OF STATE POLICY MAKING

For Offe the significance of the expansion of productive state activity is that it brings into being new and additional (decommodified) forms of social relations of production. Yet, although the commodity form depends upon the extension of these productive state activities, the latter nevertheless tend to undermine the dominance of the capital relation, and thus the conditions on which their survival depends. State productive activities not only exacerbate the financial problems of government, but open up the state to possibilities of political and social conflicts over state resources themselves.

One of the ways in which this potential conflict can be defused is through the application of technical rationality, in which political issues or practical problems are transformed into technical problems and solutions. In this way state management is given more scope in its attempts to increase the 'efficiency' of its organizations.

Offe avers, however, that because of the mode of rationality which governs state organizations, the state is unable to achieve efficiency according to its own criteria (because there is no way to determine whether efficiency or effectiveness has been advanced, and increases in efficiency are usually at the expense of effectiveness) (1975b). In Offe's view, state policies are only efficient or effective to the extent that they succeed in putting individuals in a position to find employment for their labour power, or to invest their capital profitably. To this end we find governments pursuing strategies of 'administrative recommodification', (regulations and financial incentives, public infrastructure and neo-corporatist institutions). But these measures still tend to be costly for state budgets and still 'take place under social arrangements which are themselves external to commodity relationships'.

Further strategies therefore include the reprivatization of public goods and services, motivated not only by the need to relieve the burden of taxation, but also to remove state productive activities from the political arena.

Writing in 1975, Offe claimed that policies of recommodification, privatization and retrenchment of public expenditure can only serve to undermine the basis of mass loyalty and de-politicization on which the state depends. In particular the increased visibility of the dual reference of the state's productive activities, to the commodity form on the one hand and to use-values on the other hand, can create problems of legitimation. Legitimation problems occur when expectations that a government will 'contribute to common and individual welfare and other desirable ends' fail. Offe contends that when the discrepancy between the promise and actual experience of welfare services, 'causes attitudes of frustration over false promises', then there is a possibility of the undermining of acceptance of the state's legitimacy (1975b).

Offe's concept of legitimation should however be treated with circumspection. Whilst it may yet be the case that governments ultimately have to guarantee legitimation as well as conditions of profitability, recent government policies which have not produced desirable or material outcomes have not been accompanied by a withdrawal of mass loyalty from political authority. Held has argued in his criticism of legitimation crisis that 'the worthiness of a political order to be recognised is not a necessary condition for every relatively stable society . . . what matters most is the approval of the dominant groups' (1982). Discussing the theory of legitimation crisis in relation to British society Held (1984) finds little evidence to support the claim that the state's authority or legitimacy is threatened; rather, he argues, legitimacy has never been high, political attitudes are characterized by the lack of a common value system, or general respect for or trust in the authority of the state. People's experiences at work and elsewhere are fragmented and atomized supporting a pragmatic acceptance and partial understanding of the political order. Moreover, 'the dull compulsion of economic relations' constitutes for most people an immense pressure to acquiesce. Held also notes that the thesis underestimates the extent to which the state can exercise, and in recent years has exercised, coercive and repressive measures through its monopoly control of the legitimate use of violence.

Offe's propositions may also understate state managers' capacity for directing coercive forms of control to state welfare work. These policies have created pressures of bureaucratization and intensification of work which as Weber identified are as coercive as those in private sector organizations. In this context the distinction drawn by Offe between bureaucratic and purposive rational modes of organization is less clear-cut than he suggests. The application of purposive rationality, that is techniques applied in private sector organizations, can itself lead to bureaucratic modes of organization. Thus the introduction of purposive rational techniques in the public services in Britain in the 1960s and 1970s, led to increased forms and costs of bureaucratization. For example increased bureaucratic structures developed from, firstly, the rationalization of management structures such as corporate management in local government following the Bains Report, the reorganization of management in the NHS, the establishment of Social Service Departments, and the implementation of the Salmon Report in nursing management. Second, the increased use of capital investment and centralization to achieve economies of scale. Third, the increased use of work study, work measurement and job description studies (Fryer *et al*. 1978).

More recently the fiscal and political pressures facing state managers (discussed more fully in Chapters 6 and 7) have also led them to implement a variety of forms of market rationality in state welfare organizations. Private sector styles of management, the compulsory contracting out of some services, and the use of 'efficiency' criteria have all rationalized and intensified work processes in state welfare organizations.

These more coercive forms of control highlight certain tensions which are present in state welfare work. State work does represent, as the critical writers claim, a form of production liberated from the commodity form, but this view ignores the 'factory like logic' of state institutions (Keane 1978). As Keane has argued, state production is a highly ambiguous development. Forms of social inequality are perpetuated and developed for both workers and clients, for instance, the persistence of low-paid, gendered and racial divisions of labour, and forms of stigmatism and dependency induced by professional and bureaucratic definitions of clients' 'needs'.

Nevertheless, despite the validity of the criticisms noted above, the ambiguous and contradictory nature of state work does have consequences for both managers and workers. As we argue in later chapters, many of the government's policies with respect to welfare work have had contradictory and unintended effects, have generated resistance and oppositions and produced further problems and tensions for state managers which have to be resolved. Issues of legitimacy and the need for governments to respond to a range of political pressures constitute, as Batstone *et al.* (1984) argue, 'political contingencies' which effect the strategies adopted by both state managers and workers. Such political contingencies can also be used as an important resource in the opposition tactics of trade unions and other groups, for instance by pointing to the way in which management control structures undermine and damage the social welfare purposes of the state's activities.

CONCLUSION

This chapter has argued that the theoretical framework developed by the critical theorists can provide a useful starting point for the analysis of state labour processes. The critical theorists have viewed the state's role and the increase in state employment in post-war capitalist countries as a major transformation of these societies. State workers and employees, they argue, add a new dimension to class analysis in which they are not directly implicated in conditions of exchange between capital and labour but are external yet dependent on the capital-wage-labour nexus.

Additionally state organizations and state policies for the distribution of goods and services are said to have become 'an arena of struggle' as they have been opened up by increased political demands and conflicts. However, whilst writers such as O'Connor and Gough have contributed to our understanding of the outcomes of the contradictory relationship of the state's activities to the private sector, for example, the growth of the welfare (and warfare) state, the fiscal crisis of the state and subsequent restructuring, they have not seen their task as involving a detailed analysis of state labour processes. It is here that the work of Offe is important, for he provides a framework which links a theory of the capitalist state to its internal modes of organization.

Applying the ideas developed by Offe to the state labour process, it has been argued that they provide a means of analysing the ambiguities facing state managers in devising 'appropriate' forms of control in organizations governed by non-market criteria yet dependent for their resources on capitalist production. Offe's arguments relating to the limits of state policy making were also discussed, namely that fiscal crisis and politicization tendencies lead to pressures for the recommodifiaction of certain state activities, which together with the state's inability for rational planning suggest the possibility of an eventual legitimation crisis. Although it was argued that these propositions may underestimate central managers' capacity to direct coercive forms of control to welfare organizations and to sources of resistance, as the discussions in later chapters show, this theoretical framework provides a useful means of analysing the contradictory pressures operating on the organization and control of welfare work.

NOTES

1. For example, the publications and consultative activities of the Brunel Institute of Organization and Social Studies, see E. Jacques (1978) and R. Rowbottom *et al.* (1974). For commentaries see Whittington and Bellaby (1979) and Draper and Smart (1974).
2. For Burns the collaborative system was sustained by 'commitment, trust and habits of mind and conduct inculcated by training on the job' (1981, p.31).
3. Restructuring of the welfare state here refers to 'policies to secure more efficient reproduction of the labour force, a shifting emphasis to the social control of destabilizing groups in society, raising productivity within the social services and the reprivatisation of parts of the welfare state' (Gough, 1979, p.141).

4 Gender and the Division of Labour

So far the discussion has omitted an analysis of the composition of those who occupy positions in the labour process. The danger here, as Hartmann has said, is that we have only considered the 'empty' places within the labour process without considering the 'Gender and racial hierarchies [that] determine who fills these empty places' (1979b, p.13). This chapter considers the contributions of theoretical developments in the 1970s and 1980s to the analysis of women's employment. The labour process debate, the reserve army of labour thesis and theories of segmented labour markets all made substantial contributions to the analysis of women's paid labour, but it was feminist writers who introduced the question of gender relations and gender oppression into the theoretical frameworks.

Little however has been written on the labour process which incorporates issues of race into the analysis (an exception is Phizacklea and Miles 1980), although as Thompson remarks 'given the differences between ethnic and gender stratification justice could not be done to either by assuming that the contours of the debate are identical' (1983, p.181). The following discussion therefore focuses on gender divisions of labour, but where possible reference will be made to ethnic divisions. The last section of the chapter considers changes in the employment patterns of women in the post-war period and in particular one form of employment that has become increasingly important—that of part-time work for women.

LABOUR PROCESS ANALYSIS

Braverman's work is one of the few accounts of the transformation of work under conditions of monopoly capital
which gives recognition to, and attempts to explain the emergence of the sexual division of labour. As we have seen in
Chapter 2, Braverman's discussion of the increased employment of women focuses on the rise of the universal market.
With the development of industrial capitalism, goods previously produced in the home could now be purchased with
wages. As families were increasingly unable to support themselves on the male wage, women workers were drawn from
the home and the farms into the new manufacturing industries. Associated with this process was the urbanization and
atomization of social and family life, so that functions
provided by the family in the past, such as recreation, leisure,
security and emotional needs, became commodities, as too
did the care of the young, the old, the sick and the handicapped.[1] The growth of industries and services to provide
these new commodities drew on women who found themselves undertaking similar work to that in their homes but now
under the control of capital.

Braverman makes use of Marx's concept of the industrial
reserve army; as capital moves into the newer areas in search
of profitable investment it draws on the relative surplus of
population made available through mechanization of the
older industries, and is supplemented by other sources of
labour such as ex-slaves and immigrants. Women also constitute a 'prime supplementary reservoir of labour' for the new
mass occupations and their low pay is reinforced by the vast
numbers in which they are available to capital.

Braverman's work is, though, at times inconsistent, for he
points to a division in the workforce between first, those in the
most rapidly growing labour-intensive, less mechanized and
low-waged forms of employment and second, those in the
declining higher-waged, and higher-mechanized industries.
Elsewhere, however, he argues that all wage workers are
becoming homogeneous as to lack of skill, pay and interchangeability of persons and function. This inconsistency is
compounded by his refusal to take into account forms of

worker opposition and resistance, and the ability, for example, of craft workers to use their bargaining position to gain higher wages and a more privileged position within the workforce. As Rubery (1978) argues 'all workers are threatened by the obsolescence of skills or by replacement by other equally skilled workers who are in plentiful supply', and this may induce defensive attempts on the part of trade unions to maintain divisions within the workforce, which includes the creation of job segregation by sex.

Beechy (1984) has also noted that by linking together different forms of men's and women's work as both routinized and fragmented Braverman has lost sight of some important differences between them. For example, Braverman's thesis applies most to industries where women have been introduced to do work previously done by men but have now been routinized, but his thesis does not fit so well those jobs which have never been defined as skilled and have traditionally been carried out by women, such as personal services. In addition, the thesis cannot account for types of work carried out in the welfare services which involve formal training and education, such as teaching, nursing and social work. Not all work carried out by women is unskilled or has been deskilled and this too depends on the definition of skill used. Braverman relies on a conception of skill derived from male craft work in manufacturing industries.

Nevertheless, despite these and many other criticisms, Braverman's work has been seen to be most useful in showing how the expansion of large-scale capital into the service sectors of the economy required the displacement of women from the home and into paid employment, thereby increasing the purchasing power of families and raising the demand for goods and services. Women were, therefore, available as a reserve army of labour at a time when the service sector was expanding, at low wages and in a time of labour shortage. This does not explain though why women have been a source of low wages, and for this we have to turn to the work of feminist writers and their analysis of the ways in which the sexual division of labour within the family affects women's position in the workforce.

The difficulties raised by Braverman's work, but more

specifically the invisibility of gendered work in the subsequent labour process debate, led many feminist writers to reconstruct labour process theory in ways which could more adequately account for women's subordination at work. As the CSE Sex and Class Group put it: 'the question of why it is women who fill these [low-paid and unskilled] places was not asked from within the original labour process perspective but introduced from outside, from a feminist point of view' (1982, p.85). Beechey has explained how these Marxist feminist approaches have developed;

There were two alternative versions of Marxist feminist theory proposed by people analysing women's employment and the labour process. In the first version the concept of patriarchy was introduced into the analysis of production . . . In the second version the Marxist analysis of production was broadened through an analysis of the family labour process relationship. (Beechey and Perkins 1985, p.251).

Heidi Hartmann is associated with the first of these versions. She has defined patriarchy as 'a set of social relationships between men, which have a material base, and which, though hierarchical, establish and create interdependence and solidarity among men that enable them to dominate women' (1979b, p.11). Hartmann (1979a) argued that patriarchal relationships existed before the development of capitalism, but as capitalism developed it posed new problems for men by bringing women and children into the labour force thereby threatening to destroy the family and the basis of men's power over women. Men therefore developed a number of techniques within work and the labour market which partly account for job segregation by sex; for example, the exclusionary power of male trade unions, the financial responsibility of men for their families, and the willingness of women to work for less money. Hartmann is arguing that capitalism and patriarchy are two distinct but interlocking systems which mutually accommodate each other, creating a vicious circle from which women cannot escape. The low wages of women keeps them dependent on men which in turn reinforces their subordination in the labour market.

Beechey's own work is associated with the second version identified above. She felt that capitalism and patriarchy were not two independent structures each with its own system of social relationships as Hartmann argued, but that capitalist social relationships are themselves patriarchal in form. In her analysis of the family-labour process relationship Beechey argued that women's availability as a cheap, unskilled and disposable workforce resulted from both the continuing 'needs' of capital for such a workforce and 'the sexual division of labour within the family and the familial ideology based on this which determines the conditions on which women sell their labour power and enter the world of paid work' (Beechey and Perkins 1985, p.252). In particular it is women's dependence on the male wage within the family that leads to their availability at lower wages in the labour market (Beechey 1977). The criticism of the labour process perspective was that it concentrated only on production within the workplace rather than production in the unpaid sphere of the family, where the domestic division of labour subordinates women and affects their situation in paid work.

People working within the Marxist feminist perspectives have made a number of criticisms of these early contributions, particularly with respect to the concept of patriarchy, which has been seen to involve a 'universal and trans-historical category of male dominance leaving us with little hope of change [and] . . . frequently grounded . . . in a supposed logic of biological reproduction' (Barrett 1980, p.12). Whatever the origins of patriarchy, it is clear however that patriarchal relations have a degree of independence from the development and form of capitalism; they 'precede and go beyond that context' (Barrett 1980, p.39).

Of particular importance here has been the debate about the character of male trade unionism and the growth of the ideal of the family wage; that is the earnings of a male worker which are sufficient to support a dependent family. Feminist writers agree about the consequences of the ideology of the family wage for women; it 'legitimated the division of labour by gender. It encouraged the notion that female participation in the labour force merely supplemented family income and served to justify unequal wage rates and sex segregation in the labour market' (May 1985, p.2).

Feminist writers disagree however on the historical purpose

of the family wage ideal. 'Was the family wage a vehicle for male supremacy [as Hartmann claimed] or was it, as Jane Humphries [1977] has argued, primarily an attempt by the working class to retain autonomy' (May 1985, p.2).[2] The debate however is not just academic, for it affects the ambivalence feminists have towards the trade-union movement. On the one hand the union movement has historically excluded women from membership and higher-paid and skilled work, on the other hand unionized women are better protected and paid than unorganized women, and trade unionism provides an unrealised potential for improving the position of women (see Milkman 1985, and the CSE Sex and Class Group 1982).

More recent studies of women's work within the labour process have sought to specify the particular social processes and mechanisms that have created and sustained gender divisions at work. Of importance here are occupational strategies of control and closure which take patriarchal forms as they have historically excluded women (see Chapter 5). Other studies have sought to specify the mechanisms through which skilled jobs are socially constructed and the means by which women's work is defined as unskilled. These studies do not deny that there may be a technical content to jobs defined as skilled, but rather argue that much of the work done by women also has a skill content that has been unrecognized or devalued (see Littler 1982 for strong and weak versions of the social construction theory of skill). Partly this is because women do not enter jobs which involve formal apprenticeships or long training, or have failed to get their jobs defined as skilled through trade unions. Partly it is also because women have in some occupations been excluded from skilled work by male trade unionists who have in the past been successful in getting their work defined as skilled. Cockburn (1983) for instance has described this process with respect to the printers. But many of the skills which women use at work are those which they learn informally at home and which are not defined as skilled, for example cooking, cleaning, sewing or caring work.

The social construction of skilled work has led some writers to explore the notion of 'gendered work', that is the definition of some jobs as women's work or men's work because they draw on different competencies which each sex is deemed to have. Davies and Rosser (1984) for example show how certain jobs within the administrative and clerical grades in the NHS were defined in gendered ways as they drew on 'organizational skills developed by women in household management and their experience at home·in handling emotions'. Crompton and Jones similarly found that older clerical women workers used a range of technical and social skills which arose from their experience in raising a family, yet these skills were not recognized or were devalued, and the women were paid at lower rates than men and had no possibilities of promotion (1984, p.146). The concept of gendered work also has alliances with the analysis of women's work as 'caring work', an unacknowledged and unpaid aspect of workplace labour, and particularly those jobs within welfare work which draw on skills developed through the 'invisible, devalued and privatized labour in the home' (Graham 1983).

THE INDUSTRIAL RESERVE ARMY OF LABOUR

The suggestion that women are used as a flexible and easily disposable source of labour is consistent with Marx's use of the industrial reserve army. For Marx the industrial reserve army was a permanent feature of the capitalist accumulation process. As total capital increases, less labour is required, since changes in the labour process and the application of technology can extract more labour from each worker, thereby producing a relatively redundant or surplus working population. Thus, 'the overwork of the employed part of the working class swells the ranks of the reserve' (1976, p.789). The periodic changes of high production and stagnation associated with capitalist production require the 'constant formation, greater or less absorption, and the reformation of the industrial reserve army' (1976, p.785). Marx identifies three forms of the reserve army: the floating, the latent and the stagnant.

The floating form exists in the centres of modern industry where workers are sometimes repelled and sometimes attracted; this is often associated with the substitution of younger workers for older ones, or less skilled for skilled workers. The latent form is the agricultural population which is drawn into the surplus population when capitalist production penetrates agriculture.

The stagnant form is the casual, irregular, pauperized, and inexhaustible reservoir of disposable labour power found amongst those expelled from industry and who find it difficult to gain employment.

Beechey (1978) has noted that the reserve army serves several functions for capital in Marx's work. It provides a disposable and flexible population which can be absorbed when there is a demand and repelled when not wanted; it produces competition between workers which can depress wage levels; workers submit to an increase in exploitation through pressure of unemployment; and it counteracts the tendency for the rate of profit to fall. Beechey suggests that although women are not given much attention by Marx, they can nevertheless be included in the reserve army, as along with men they can be repelled from either modern industry or agriculture. However, she argues that the reserve army is a long-term general term, and does not differentiate between the different employment of women in different industries and at different periods. Nor, as Barrett notes, does the thesis of the reserve army tell us 'why it should be women who necessarily occupy a particular place in it', unless the conditions which make women available as workers are also specified (1980, p.159).

Beechey shows that it is the sexual division of labour which confines women to the family, and the patriarchal ideology embodied in it, which gives certain advantages to capital in employing female labour, especially married women. She asks whether married women constitute a specific form of the industrial reserve army which is different from the forms described by Marx, and contends that married women do function as a cheaper, disposable and flexible labour force as a result of their domestic role in the family. Married women are less strongly unionized, are more horizontally mobile, and willing to take on part-time work because of domestic responsibilities; they receive fewer state benefits and in addition disguise the extent of unemployment since they 'disappear virtually without trace back into the family', and lastly they are less likely to qualify for redundancy money. In an earlier paper she also developed the argument that women are available at lower wages because they are dependent on the male wage within the family (1977).

There is however an inconsistency in this analysis which other writers have noted. If women are employed because they are a cheap source of labour they may be less likely to be made redundant in times of recession than the more expensive male workers. This negates the thesis that women are part of an industrial reserve army, which predicts that they would be the most disposable in times of recession (Barrett 1980, Walby 1985). It has also been argued that the sex-segregated nature of the workforce and the concentration of women in particular sectors also militates against the reserve army thesis, for segregation will protect women from expulsion in times of declining demand for labour (Milkman 1976). Barrett put this simply: 'if all typists and cleaners are female (which is virtually the case) it is implausibe to suggest that they can all be dispensed with' (1980, p.161). This criticism of the industrial reserve army led Breugal to argue that women's concentration in the service industries protected them from redundancies in the 1970s and 1980s (Breugal 1979).

More recently, Humphries (1983), has argued that women have formed part of the industrial reserve in historically specific ways, namely, initially in the post-war period women were part of the latent reserve, since capitalist production penetrated home production releasing women to join the labour force. In America now, however, there is evidence to suggest that women have been assimilated into the labour force and are increasingly being substituted for male workers.[3] We return to these arguments in Section three, where changes in women's employment patterns, employers' use of part-time female workers and the implications for the reserve army thesis are discussed.

Migrant labour in the economies of Western capitalist societies in the post-war period has also served as an industrial reserve army in addition to being, as we discuss below, an important element in the secondary labour market. In the

USA the influx of large numbers of migrants from Mexico and the Caribbean countries since the 1960s has been a source of an 'infinite reserve army' (Davis 1984a, p.29), and their race/ethnic status has confined them to the growing low-waged, labour-intensive service industries especially in the sunbelt states. In northern Europe migrant labour has been recruited from the less developed countries, from Turkey, Greece, southern Italy, and from former colonies, and drawn into the economies in the 1960s, contributing to economic growth of these countries during that period (Castles and Kosack 1973, Kindleberger 1967). In the 1970s, as economic growth declined and the social costs of migrant families increased, many of these countries, but in particular those who had drawn most heavily on migrants—West Germany, Switzerland and France—discharged the migrant workers, especially those who were employed for limited periods of time.

Migrant labour clearly played an important role in introducing flexibility into the rigidities of indigenous labour markets since migrants could be hired, used and then discharged according to economic fluctuations. However, despite the return of the 'Gästarbeiter' to their own countries, and more restrictive immigration policies, there still remain high numbers of foreign workers in the major countries of Europe, their social and economic relationships marked by racism and a lack of civil, political, social and industrial rights. In Britain migrant workers before 1971 were not excluded from citizen's rights but their employment and domestic opportunities have remained distinguished from those of the indigenous population by forms of institutional and individualized racism.

Doyal *et al.'s* (1981) study of migrant workers in the NHS in Britain shows first that in industry generally migrant workers have been employed in various ways by employers to counter the tendency of rate of profit to fall. This involved sometimes keeping down the costs of labour, but in other cases migrant workers were used to facilitate technological change and rationalization. Second, they show how in the NHS migrant workers were recruited as a source of cheap labour to fill posts which were least attractive to the indigenous population. Migrant workers are, therefore, to be found disproportionately in the unskilled, low-paid jobs in the NHS particularly in the ancillary services where in some parts of the country migrant labour constitutes a very high proportion of ancillary posts. Doyal's study found that over 80% of ancillaries in a London hospital were from abroad, the majority of whom were women. Migrant workers also constitute a high percentage of doctors and nurses but they are usually concentrated in subordinate and unpopular positions within these professions.

Doyal *et al.* further argue that migrant workers as ancillaries and nurses have also facilitated the reorganizations and rationalizations of work which have been imposed within the health service since the 1960s. Work permits for ancillary workers from abroad have now been stopped in line with the government policy of tightening immigration controls, so that this source of labour is no longer available to health authorities. They now however recruit in substantial numbers part-time married women workers or, in those areas where migrants have settled, black British women workers.

DUAL AND SEGMENTED LABOUR MARKETS

Attempts to explain the structure of rewards and opportunities of different groups in the economy have come from theories of labour market segmentation. Divisions within the workforce by race, sex, educational credentials and industrial groupings are seen to 'operate within different labour markets, with different working conditions, different promotional opportunities, different wages and different market institutions' (Reich, Gordon, and Edwards 1973). Earlier theories were developed in the United States by economists as a means of explaining the persistence of poverty and subemployment of disadvantaged groups in the large American cities. Two sets of theories emerged: the dual labour market theory of Doeringer and Piore (1971) and segmented labour market theory of Reich, Gordon, and Edwards (1973).

In the 1950s Kerr used the concept of the 'balkanization' of internal labour markets to describe the development of a sheltered sector confined to the plant, craft or industrial groups. These internal markets were characterized by firm specific skills, on the job training, defined ports of entry to jobs, job security, and governed by institutional and formal rules negotiated between management and unions rather than individual employer preferences. Kerr contrasted the structured nature of management–labour relations in such internal labour markets with the unstructured nature of non-unionized employment relations.

Following Kerr, Doeringer and Piore described the labour market as being divided into the primary and the secondary sectors, each characterized by the nature of the jobs and workers. The primary sector offers jobs with high wages, good working conditions, promotion prospects, employment security, and equity and due process in the administration of work rules. In turn, workers in this sector tend to have firm specific skills, and stable work habits. A distinction was made, however, between independent primary and subordinate primary workers. Independent primary workers have professional or higher qualifications and can pursue career paths between firms, while subordinate primary workers have fewer formal qualifications, are found in the routinized non-manual or manual jobs, and follow career paths within the firm. Internal labour markets are, therefore, to be found mainly in this subordinate primary sector. Secondary sector jobs were characterized as being low-paid, with poor working conditions, little chance of promotion, arbitrary supervision, employment instability and high labour turnover. Secondary jobs discourage the development of stable work habits, or the learning of skills.

The main determinants of a dual labour market are, for Doeringer and Piore, the emergence of large, stable product markets and technological developments. In these conditions employers need to form a stable workforce and can offer them wages and conditions above the external market rates. Negotiation between management and unions also contributes to better conditions of work and wages and the emergence of internal labour markets. In the unstable secondary sector, however, employers need to be able to adjust their workforce quickly to fluctuations of demand for their product and hence require a workforce that can be hired and fired with greater ease.

The radical economists, Edwards, Gordon and Reich accepted the stratified labour market hypothesis put forward by Doeringer and Piore, but preferred to describe it as a segmented labour market to refer to more than just two divisions within the workforce. For these writers, however, segmented labour markets arise out of the political and economic forces within American capitalism and, in particular, the transition from competitive to monopoly capitalism. In this analysis employers actively and consciously devised strategies to break down the more homogeneous workforce that emerged with the development of large factory production. 'Employers aimed to divide the labour force into various segments so that the actual experiences of workers were different and the basis of their common opposition to capitalists undermined'. In addition segmentation was intensified by the growth of both large capital-intensive, monopolistic firms and the small, competitive and labour-intensive firms. As Doeringer and Piore had proposed, a dualism of working environments, wages and mobility patterns emerged between the two sectors. Labour market segmentation was seen to be functional in several ways; first, it prevents potential movements uniting all workers against employers; second, as workers perceive barriers to mobility they limit their own aspirations; and third, inequalities in authority and control between superiors and subordinates, for example, male and female workers or white and black workers, are legitimized.

These earlier theories of stratified labour markets have, however, been shown to be over-simplified and flawed in a number of respects. Rubery argues that the theories present a rationalization of the present structure of the American labour market, rather than an explanation of how this was arrived at. The theories are difficult to apply to the analysis of labour markets outside the United States and this, Rubery suggests, is because of the 'almost exclusive attention paid to the actions and motivations of the capitalists in developing a structured labour market, and the consequent neglect of the role of worker organizations in the process' (1978). As we discuss in Chapter 6, in comparison with America, unionization in Britain was more strongly and widely established before the emergence of the large corporations, and probably played a more important role in the development of structured labour markets. Thus unions in Britain were able to exert considerable control over entry to occupations, manning levels, craft demarcations, and could resist the introduction of new technologies more successfully.

In their more recent work, however, Gordon, Edwards, and Reich (1982) do take into account the role of unions in their historical analysis of the structuring of labour markets and changes in the organization of work in the USA. They propose that there have been three overlapping stages in the development of the labour process and labour markets in the US since the nineteenth century, of which labour segmentation represents the third of these transformations. These stages are (i) initial proletarianization from the 1820s to the 1890s, in which a workforce of wage workers was created; (ii) a period of homogenization from the 1870s to the onset of World War II, in which jobs were deskilled and control over the labour process passed to employers; and (iii) segmentation of labour from the 1920s to the present, in which employers responded to the militancy of the unions in the 1930s and immediate post-war period by encouraging internal labour markets and the integration of the unions into a collective bargaining structure. The clear divisions which have since developed between the unionized and non-unionized sectors of the American economy have resulted in the segmented primary and secondary labour markets described above (see also Chapter 6).

Such segmentation has played 'a major role in channelling the effects of past and present race and sex discrimination' (p. 16). Gordon, Edwards and Reich show, for example, how, in the US, four developments in particular have resulted in segmented patterns of female employment in the post-war period. First, corporate demand for clerical workers has been filled largely by women, but employers have segregated male and female jobs within white-collar occupations, so that women, and particularly married women, are channelled into the subordinate primary jobs with little chances of promotion, and men are retained for those jobs with promotion. Second, the expansion of the state service sector has given women increased employment in, for example, health and education, but in subordinate occupations that are extensions of women's traditional female role. Thirdly and fourthly, women have increased their employment in the low-paying and unstable sectors of peripheral manufacturing industries such as transportation and communication and peripheral services such as the retail trade. These developments accounted for 95% of all female employment in 1970 (p.206).

Whilst the theory of labour market segmentation has made an important contribution to the analysis of the subordinate work position of women and minorities, the work of Gordon *et al.* has been criticised on the grounds that they do not take into account discriminatory practices between male and female workers or white and black workers, nor do they consider the importance of ideology in the shaping of perceptions of both employers and employees, for example the way in which women's opportunities at work are affected by familial ideology. Kendrick points out for instance that the radical economists only refer to segmentation as a 'technique of employer control, and pre-existing race and sex divisions are used as an additional resource in a strategy of divide and rule'. The authors do not refer 'to conflicts between workers and the benefits they derive themselves from discriminatory practices [on grounds of race and sex]' (1981, p.172). As mentioned earlier, one way in which conflicts between male and female workers has been analysed by feminist writers is in the debate on the family wage ideal. Humphries (1977) showed that in Britain the unions historically used defensive strategies to secure a 'family wage', and that this involved union resistance to the employment of women, whom they felt would lower the level of wages. In turn however the notion of a family wage is used to legitimize 'pin money' wages to female workers.

This and other critiques of the earlier theories have now been incorporated into 'second generation models' of segmented labour markets (Rubery *et al.* 1984). Important here have been contributions which focus on the supply-side of the labour that, that is the social reproduction of labour. Social reproduction differs between countries but includes: the family structure, the structure of waged and non-waged work, the role of the state in the reproduction of the labour force and social and political organizations of waged and non-waged labour (Mercato 1981). Recognition is given not just to sexual divisions of labour but also to the political and ideological influences that promote this and other divisions of labour. Thus for example, wage levels may be linked to the individual's position in the social reproductive system, so that older, younger and female workers are available at lower wages because of their reliance on other workers in their families or on the state. This cheap labour supply can then be used by capital in a number of ways, for example to keep firms from going out of business or in struggles against organized labour in the introduction of new technology. Important too are ideological influences of perceptions of domestic responsibilities and the division of labour within the home, which affect employers' views of appropriate work for particular groups and the way in which members of these groups may perceive their role.

CHANGING EMPLOYMENT PATTERNS

The characteristics of women's entry into paid work are well known. In Britain between 1961 and 1981, women as a proportion of the workforce increased from 35% to 40%. Married women in particular have entered the labour market in increasingly large numbers, their economic activity rate changing from 29.7% in 1961 to 48.8% in 1981 (Equal Opportunities Commission 1981). Women however are concentrated in industries and occupations that are predominantly female, for example women comprise over 70% of the labour force in two main occupations: clerical and related, and catering, cleaning, hairdressing and other personal services, and almost 70% in education, welfare and health. Hakim (1981) has referred to this segregation as horizontal occupational segregation, that is, men and women are most commonly working in different types of occupation. Martin and Roberts' (1984) survey of women's employment, for example, found that two-thirds of women were in jobs occupied only by women. Vertical segregation also exists as men are commonly working in higher-grade occupations and women in the lower grades of non-manual work, or the semi and unskilled grades of manual work.

In the USA women now comprise 43% of the labour force, and the proportion of women working has grown from 43% in 1960 to 63% in 1986 (OECD 1986). The sex-segregated nature of the occupational structure is also evident as about 80% of women work in 25 of the 420 occupations identified by the US Department of Labor. In many of these jobs women are working with women only, for example about 99% of secretaries, 85% of registered nurses, 82% of librarians and 86% of clerks are women (Koziara 1985).

Associated with the entry of women into the paid labour force in the post-war years have been marked changes in the industrial and occupational composition of the workforce. First there has been the shift from manufacturing jobs to service employment of which the expansion of state jobs has been an important component. In Britain manufacturing employment fell by nearly two and a half million between 1966 and 1981. Urry has remarked that 'Since 1970, whilst most economies have experienced jobless growth, in manufacturing, Britain first experienced a period of job destroying growth, then one of job destroying zero growth and finally one of job destroying manufacturing collapse' (1983, p.35). As he points out this implies both the growth, relatively and absolutely, of service employment and large increases in unemployment.

In contrast the USA has added thirty-two million jobs to the economy since 1960, but has also experienced a decline in manufacturing jobs and a growth in service jobs in the private sector, especially health care, business services and fast food.[4] These industrial shifts are associated with spatial relocations as capital has moved to the southern and south-western 'sun-belt' states, and although almost a million manufacturing jobs were lost in the northern states in the 1970s, some new jobs in manufacturing were created in the south. But the main growth of employment has been amongst women and migrant workers in low-waged service jobs. Rothschild (1981) has noted that 'between 1972 and 1980 women accounted for 65% of the employment rise—an amount disproportionate to their 38% share of employment in 1972'; most of this growth has occurred in industries that paid below the average wage.[5]

Much of the growth of service employment in the post-war period is also associated with the expansion of public sector employment, and in particular the growth of social welfare (until political pressures brought a halt in the late 1970s—see Chapter 6). As Rein shows, the increase in social welfare jobs accounted for 48% of the growth of women's employment in the US in the post-war period, and 56% of the growth of women's employment in Britain (1985).

A second development has involved changes in employment practices. In the face of intense international competition for declining markets and macro-economic policies of governments at home, industries have been forced to reorganize, relocate or close production facilities (the spatial effects of these developments in Britain are described briefly in Chapter 6). As a result employment policies have been changing at an unprecedented rate during the 1980s as employers have shed workers, rationalized production, introduced new technology or devised new employment packages to increase the flexibility and productivity of workers. It has therefore been argued that the changing organization of work is increasingly characterized by segmentation into core and peripheral groups of workers each with their own terms and conditions of employment (Atkinson 1985).

Thus Brown has noted that the core workers are presented with an employment package of 'training and payment practices that elicit high labour efficiency through the . . . route of cultivating commitment' (1986, p.163). At the other extreme employers seek to obtain a relatively cheap and easily disposable workforce, either through subcontracting, fixed contract or self-employment on specialist projects, or by direct employment of workers who are denied career status, or who are part-time, temporary or casual workers. It has been anticipated that there will be increasing growth in the periphery and a decline in the core with a growing polarization between the two forms of labour.

Evidence does now suggest that in both the USA and the UK, as in a number of other industrial capitalist countries, the number of full-time, relatively well-paid and unionized jobs has been declining, and is being replaced by feminized, low-paid, part-time and non-unionized jobs in the service sector. Davis notes, with regard to the United States, that 'low wage employment far from being a mere "periphery" to a high wage core, has become the job growth pole of the economy' (Davis 1984a, p.19). Humphries (1983) argues that although women as the newest workers initially occupied secondary employment, there is now evidence to suggest that in the United States, because of their relatively lower wages, they are increasingly being substituted for male primary jobs in industry. The restructuring of jobs in the US has meant the decline of 'tough' male jobs in the basic industries and an expansion of low-paid and feminized work.

In Britain there has also been a growth of the peripheral sector of employment, for example in 1985 one and a half million workers were on temporary or fixed-term contracts, and self-employment rose from 7.4% of the workforce in 1978 to 10.8% in 1985. In Britain most of the rise in labour market participation since the early 1950s has been through increasing numbers of married women returning to work in part-time jobs. Part-time jobs rose from 15% of employment in 1971 to 25% in 1985. As part-time employment is such an important form of women's employment it is to a more detailed discussion of this that we now turn.

PART-TIME WORK

In Britain, between 1961 and 1984, part-time female employment rose from just under two million to four million, that is from 26% of all female workers to 44%. During the same period the proportion of male and female full-time employees declined. Of those who work part-time in Britain, the vast majority (88%) are women, of whom three quarters are married women *(Employment Gazette,* May 1985).[6]

In the US the proportion of part-time workers in the labour force has also been growing, from 15% of non-agricultural jobs in 1954 to 22% in 1983. Women also comprise a high proportion of part-time workers (66%) though this is a smaller proportion than in the UK. However, fewer married women in the US work part-time than in Britain, for as Dex

states 'American women work far more than British women—
and in full-time jobs—over their family formation period'.
Dex has explained this difference by examining child-care
constraints in the two countries. 'US women work full time,
pay for child care and get tax deductions against child care
expenses. British women have to work part-time and get
husbands or relatives to care for young children' (1985,
pp.5-6).

In Britain, as in the US, part-time work is concentrated in
the service industries in both the private and public sectors of
the economy. In the services generally, more than 80% of all
women part-time workers in the distribution, insurance,
banking, finance and business services, professional and
scientific, miscellaneous (pubs, hairdressers) and public
administration services. In the public services, and especially
welfare services, there has been a disproportionate rise in
part-time work compared to the private sector, so that now
about half of women who work in social welfare are part-time,
compared to 38% in the private sector (Rein 1985). Most of
the growth in public sector part-time employment occurred in
the early 1970s, but between 1978 and 1984, although there
had been a slight decline in both full-time and part-time
employment for men, women's part-time employment had
continued to increase (Economic Trends 1983 and 1985). A
large proportion of part-time work in the services is manual,
and in the public services it is domestic work or unqualified
teaching, nursing and social work, concentrated in jobs in the
lowest grades. Associated with part-time work is significant
downward occupational mobility for women returning to
work after childbirth.[7]

It is often assumed that part-time employment exists
because it is a form of employment preferred and chosen by
women with child-care and domestic responsibilities. Recent
studies have suggested, rather, that part-time work is a form
of employment demanded by employers because it enables
flexibility of labour use, and is a source of cheap labour
(Perkins 1983, Mallier and Rosser 1979, Robinson and
Wallace 1984). In other words employers have chosen to offer
part-time jobs rather than recruit full-time female workers.
At a national level this has occurred despite an adequate

availability of full-time workers, and studies of particular localities, such as Perkins' study of Coventry, found there was no shortage of female full-time workers to explain the expansion of part-time work. Mallier and Rosser have also suggested that changes in employment legislation in 1975 made it more favourable for employers to recruit part-time workers, since until 1983 they could be paid at a lower rate than full-timers, and under sixteen hours a week were excluded from the protective employment rights.

Married women with children, however, are attracted to part-time work because the reduced hours enable them to supplement child-care responsibilities and household care with paid work. As Coyle points out though, the cost of part-time working for women has been enormous, 'it has made it possible for women to be wage earners and domestic labourers without there having been any real redistribution of domestic work between men and women. As a result, women have remained defined in terms of the domestic and through this are structured as a secondary, marginal and subordinate labour force' (1984).

Explanations of the increased importance of part-time work as a form of employment have come from the application of Marx's reserve army of labour thesis to the analysis of female employment. Breugal (1979), for example, has argued that part-time women workers do fit the reserve army thesis since in the period 1974-1978 a higher proportion of them lost their jobs, especially in the declining manufacturing industries, although women in the service sector were to some extent protected by the general expansion in this sector. Perkins (1983) in her study of Coventry, doubts, however, that part-time women are necessarily the most disposable part of the workforce for she found that they are now used as a permanent and essential part of the overall organization of labour. In manufacturing industries in the 1970s part-timers were used for labour flexibility by employers, and full-timers emerged as the group which were most disposable since they led to greater reductions in labour costs. The permanent use of part-time staff meant that they could be used as a cheap form of overtime labour and as a group of experienced workers who could fill in for sickness and holiday periods, obviating the need for expensive and unreliable temporary and casual labour.

In the service industries too Perkins found that the permanent employment of part-time women as a cheaper and more flexible workforce was the typical form of employment, rather than the most disposable form. This is confirmed at a national level, as Dex and Perry in a review of women's employment patterns in the 1970s also found that part-time work rarely decreased from year to year and overall there had been a substitution of female part-time work for women full-time workers and male full- and part-time workers (1984).

In the public sector, women's part-time employment has continued to grow as other components of employment have started to decline in the 1980s (Dex and Perry 1984), which suggests also that part-time work does not constitute the most disposable part of employment.[8] Part-time employment in the public services has grown because of demand by employers to keep down wage costs in a labour-intensive industry, or to match fluctuations in operational requirements, such as school dinner or patient meal times (Robinson and Wallace 1984). In the last few years public sector employers have increased their numbers of both part-time and temporary staff because of the uncertainties imposed on these agencies by staffing cuts and the impending privatization of some services. Employers can then use part-timers to increase their flexibility to make short-term changes.[9]

Where tenders in the contracting-out process have gone to private contractors there is excessive use of part-time working, with often the majority of workers working below sixteen hours per week (and therefore not being entitled to protective employment benefits) and with high ratios of part-time staff to full-time (NUPE 1985; 1986). However, as we discuss in Chapter 8, irrespective of whether a contract is won in-house or by a private company, the effect of the contract is to segment the workforce by casualizing and marginalizing the terms and conditions of employment for the contract workers. This particularly affects the wages, work processes and conditions of employment for women, since domestic ancillary work is predominantly work done by women.

Although flexibility of labour is one reason why employers recruit women to part-time jobs, Beechey and Perkins have also argued that there are gender-specific ways in which employers organize their workforce—the question of gender must also be brought into the analysis of part-time employment. In their own research into part-time work in the public services, the authors stress the role of family ideology. They argue that 'domestic and unqualified caring work in the public services has been constructed in such a way that it replicates women's domestic role within the home'. They state:

The major part of the reason why so much domestic work is part time is because it is women's work. In employing women to do jobs which are similar to those performed, unpaid, within the home, managements make use of gender specific skills which women have learned informally at home, yet the women's jobs are generally not classified as skilled (1985, p.259).

Employers then have perceptions of what kind of work is appropriate for women with domestic responsibilities and have found that the restricted job choice of married women who need hours to fit in with domestic and child-care responsibilities is a ready source of recruitment for part-time hours.

This evidence on part-time employment suggests then that employers have used part-time labour in a variety of different ways and for a variety of reasons, and not just as the most easily disposable part of the labour force. The evidence does though present problems for the analysis of women's employment as part of an industrial reserve army since this thesis would predict that they are the most disposable part of the labour force. Rather, the studies discussed above suggest that women should be seen as permanently attached to the labour force. As Dex (1985) comments, conventional concepts have not proved adequate to the analysis of women's employment, and more specific gender-related questions need to be formulated for both men's and women's work.

NOTES

1. There is in this account, as Beechey (1982) has noted, a romanticized and ahistorical view of the family which has similarities with the structural functional accounts of industrialization and the family.
2. Barrett and McIintosh (1980) take the view that in the nineteenth century there was a coincidence of interests between bourgeois philanthropists and the state on the one hand and the emergent Chartist and trade-union movement on the other which led to the Factory Acts in Britain and the limitation of the length of the working day and a reduction in child and female labour. May's (1985) own view is that the family wage appeared first as a class demand, as a solution to the threats that a working man perceived to himself and his family in the new industrial order. Later, the family wage demand took the form of female exclusion, as unionism developed and social reformers and progressive activists took up the issue as a solution to instability within the working-class family.
3. Humphries (1983) has criticized the identification of the industrial reserve army with cyclical variations in employment as too restrictive, and suggests that a longer time perspective is required in which women are substituted for men, as part of female proletarianization in the post-war period. She argues that Marx's account of the industrial reserve army was historically specific, for whilst the latent form of the reserve did apply to the rise in female participation rates in the post-war period, 'in the 1980s, the identification of women workers with a latent industrial reserve is anachronistic' (p.14). Since World War II women have formed part of the latent reserve, as capitalist production has penetrated home production, releasing women to join industrial production. According to Humphries this occurred initially 'as a result of expanding demand in "feminized" sectors', but more recently because the wife's income was necessary if a family was to remain above the poverty level (1983, p.14 and Humphries and Rubery 1984). 'There is no slack on the household economy capable of absorbing a large scale retreat of women workers'. The exhaustion of the latent reserve means that first, capital has to create such a reservoir elsewhere, the obvious target being Third World countries with their own relative surplus populations' (p.14), and second, women workers are now being assimilated into the labour force and in the US are increasingly being substituted for men.
4. J. Singleman and M. Tienda (1985) show that manufacturing (mining and transformative) industries declined from 36.7% of US employment in 1960 to 30.7% in 1980. In the recession of the 1980s goods-producing industries lost 800,000 jobs between 1980 and 1984. In the private sector Davis (1984a) notes that for each new job added in goods production between 1966 and 1981, ten were added in the tertiary sector (minus the state sector). Davis (1984a) also shows that in the private service sector growth was disproportionately concen-

trated in three industries: health services, business services and fast food; as he vividly puts it 'McDonalds now employs more workers than the entire American basic steel industry' (Davis 1984a, p.24).

5. Wages in the private sector averaged $9,853 in 1979; in the industrial sector they averaged $21,433. In nursing and personal services, in which 89% of workers are women, the average wage in 1979 was $3.87 per hour compared with $16.16 in the entire private economy (Rothschild 1981, pp.12-14).

6. In examining the official statistical evidence on the employment of women, some caution should be used, for much of the data is conceptualized, collected and presented in such a way as to render women less visible than men. Social statistics are socially constructed, and as Hunt (1980) has argued, government employment statistics embody a masculine conception of employment, in that female patterns of employment are not presented or are under-recorded. The data on part-time work from the Census of Employment, New Earnings Survey, and Census of Production, all underestimate the extent of part-time employment. The Census of Employment includes only those employees in employment as opposed to the 'economically active'—the latter classification would include more women—and employers are also asked to give information for one particular week of the year, which therefore underrepresents seasonal and casual work, a characteristic of part-time work. The New Earnings Survey is based on PAYE income-tax records, which exclude many low-paid workers, who are often part-time, and not liable for tax. The Labour Force Survey, which collects data comparable to EEC countries, does collect data on the 'economically active', but uses one particular week in the year, and as with all small samples is subject to sampling error. The Census of Production includes only manufacturing industries, in which only one third of women are employed. We do not therefore have a comprehensive picture of women's, and especially their part-time, employment patterns. More recently, studies of women's employment patterns have been carried out which attempt to redress the deficiencies of government statistics by reconceptualizing forms and patterns of employment which more closely fit those of women. Recent examples of these are Martin and Roberts' (1984) study of a sample of 10,000 women and Beechey and Perkins (1985) study of part-time work.

In addition to the difficulties noted above, what constitutes part-time work also poses problems, for in Britain there are different definitions in employment legislation, in official statistics, for benefit purposes and in collective agreements (Labour Research Department 1986). There are also difficulties in comparisons between different countries, in that the United States makes a distinction between voluntary and involuntary part-time work, the latter applying to workers who are temporarily on short time for economic reasons. This distinction is not made in Britain or in the European Labour Force Survey.

7. Martin and Roberts' study (1984) found that in their sample of women workers the majority of part-time workers within the service sector (70%) worked in manual jobs. This survey also found that part-time work was associated with a significant downward mobility of women returning to work after childbirth. In the public services over 90% of all jobs classified in the lowest grades were held by part-time female employees (Robinson and Wallace 1984).

8. For example, between September 1985 and September 1986 the Joint Manpower Watch figures recorded a decrease in full-time staff for local authorities by 4,577 and an increase in part-time staff of 13,185 (Douglas and Lord 1986).

9. In the 1980s two patterns of employment in local authorities have been discerned: first, the non-metropolitan counties had reduced part-time jobs because they were easier to cut, and second, metropolitan counties had substituted part-time for full-time staff (Travers quoted in Webster 1985).

5 The Professions, the State and the Structuring of Work

This chapter considers the implications of the expansion of professional and higher-level workers in the division of labour in the post-war period. State employment in particular has been an important source of growth of professional workers. Some welfare professionals retain considerable degrees of technical autonomy, the ability to define and determine clients' needs and treatments and a role in policy determination. By no means can their work processes be seen as analogous to those of industrial workers, nor even subject to the deskilling and loss of control which Braverman and others have described as central to the proletarianization of wage workers. Other occupational groups and the semi-professions are, though, more vulnerable to the extension of managerial controls or subordination by the established professions. Section one of this chapter examines the different and conflicting interpretations of the work processes of professional workers.

In the second section of the chapter the social processes which have shaped divisions of labour amongst the professional workforce are examined through the concepts of occupational control and closure. Important here are strategies which have structured sexual divisions of labour between the established professions and the semi-professions and between management and semi-professional groups. The third section of the chapter considers professional groups in relation to the state and argues that the mutual compliance and dependence between the state and the professional providers has led to selective privileging and sponsorship of some professions and the pursuit of that sponsorship by other occupational groups. These processes have also been important in shaping divisions of labour both between professions and within professional occupations.

THEORIES OF PROFESSIONAL WORK

The expansion of the 'intermediate' strata of professionals and highly-educated labour in the twentieth century has led to a number of different and conflicting interpretations of their work and class situation. The literature is extensive, especially of the class location of educated labour, and it is not possible to review within this one chapter (see for example Abercrombie and Urry 1983 and Wright 1985),[1] rather the following discussion examines two alternative images of the transformation of work of professional workers which can be discerned in the literature. First, following Durkheim's optimism with regard to professional occupations, a long tradition in the sociological literature has maintained that professional labour occupies a privileged position in the social division of labour and has a benign influence on society. In the last two decades, though, this image of professionals as a moral and progressive force within society has come under increasing criticism as the nature of their power and monopoly control of knowledge has been widely examined.

A second image of the growth of professionalism focuses on the transformation of professionals from independent practitioners to salaried employees. Following Braverman's discussion of the middle layers of employment, arguments have concerned the proletarianization of professional workers who are increasingly subject to the constraints of managerial authority and control. Thus attention has been given to the transformation of the labour process as professional work has been intensified, subject to fragmentation and routinization, or as professional goals are subordinated to managerial goals and policies.

The first image of the growth of professional occupations asserts their primacy in the occupational structure. As Freidson remarks: 'Until recently it was common for some of the most notable scholars of the day to emphasise the importance of professions in modern society and to consider professionalism to be a major social movement transforming both society and the nature of work (1976, p.14). Writers such as Carr-Saunders and Wilson (1964), Marshall (1963) and Parsons (1958) saw professionalism as a benign and progressive movement 'which is of special importance to the effective and humane functioning of modern society' (Freidson 1976, p.14). More recently Bell has taken up this theme in his book *The Coming of Post Industrial Society* (1973). Bell argues that the shift to a service economy from a goods manufacturing economy, and the growth and predominance of professional, scientific and technical groups, have meant that theoretical knowledge is the 'strategic resource' of the post-industrial society and the source of innovation and policy formation. The major class of the emerging post-industrial society is a professional class based on knowledge which displaces the class of industrialists of the old industrial order whose power was based on the ownership of private property.

As many writers have pointed out, Bell's writing demonstrates the dangers of extrapolating future trends from one brief period and location, namely, the west coast of America during the relative economic prosperity of the 1960s. Whilst there have been important shifts in the industrial structure and in the nature of employment and work, the manufacturing industries have declined, service industries have expanded and there has been employment growth at the top and bottom of the occupational hierarchy; it is doubtful whether these developments can adequately be conceptualized in terms of a post-industrial society (Gershuny 1978, Giddens 1973, Kumar 1978). This is not to deny the increased importance of scientific and technical knowledge in the production process, but rather to suggest that these trends represent the continuation of the application of technical rationality identified in the classical theories of Marx and Weber.

Freidson too asserts the growing significance and power of knowledge-based occupations in the production process, but he distinguishes between the dominant 'key' professions established in the nineteenth century and the emerging technical (or semi-) professions of the twentieth century (1976). He considers that the latter have few prospects because

they are part of productive domains that are already organized and controlled by (i) the dominant professionals and their allies and (ii) managerial agents of either the state or corporate capital. In . . . health, welfare, law and education, . . . technical workers are organised around the delineating and supervising authority of the key professions. When they are licensed, certified or registered the legitimacy, even the legality of their work hinges upon their nominal supervision . . . They are thus bound into an occupationally subordinate position (1976, p.25).

Freidson misses, however, the significance that the semi-professions of the twentieth century are feminized occupations, so that as well as technical divisions of labour there are also sexual divisions of labour between the professions and between management and the semi-professions.

In the last two decades a view of professionalism has emerged which still considers professionals to have a dominant role in contemporary society, but the earlier image of professionals as a moral and progressive force within society has come under increasing criticism. The ability of professionals to protect their own self-interests, maintaining economic and social privileges and a monopoly of knowledge, has led to a widespread examination of the nature of power that they hold (for example Illich 1977, Foucault 1979, Esland 1980, Wilding 1982). The professions have therefore been held to exercise monopoly power in the production of certain kinds of knowledge and in definitions of clients' needs, treatments, and problems. In Smith's (1980) account people are processed through welfare bureaucracies in such a way as to make a client's 'needs' a professional and administrative accomplishment. 'Needs' are therefore seen as socially constructed by the ideological and practical activities of welfare professionals and workers. Welfare professionals also define and impose criteria of 'normality', 'deviance', or personal 'adequacy' which, as many critics have pointed out, stigmatize and make dependent welfare clients. Foucault for example has examined the emergence of the 'swarm of normative judges, teachers, psychologists, psychiatrists, and social workers who would differentiate, quantify, and rank an individual according to his abilities to conform to the normative requisites of disciplinary technologies' (Hewitt 1983, p.69).

Particularly damaging has been the feminist critique of the welfare professions and their treatment and advice to women which has reinforced gender divisions by perpetuating a stereotyped view of women's caring role within the family, and control of those who 'deviate' from this stereotype.[2] Literature from both the United States and Britain has shown that doctors have successfully 'medicalized' most of the events in women's lives—childbirth, conception, menstruation— and that the use of technology has alienated women from their bodies. Whilst most of the literature refers to the medical profession there is evidence that social work practice also reinforces the expectations that women should be 'good' wives and mothers and are the natural unpaid carers for dependent people. Yet, as many of these critiques point out, state welfare services present a paradox for women, for 'as well as being a system for reproducing patriarchal values and controlling women's sexuality [welfare services are] also a resource' (Ungerson 1985, p.151, see also Doyal 1983). The cutbacks in welfare services have therefore been seen primarily as affecting women as the main users of the services and as welfare workers.

The critique of professional power has been developed by those on both the left and the right of the political spectrum. Both consider that professionals represent ideologically powerful groups in modern society and that in their mode of intervention through bureaucratic services they have created more problems than they have solved. For those on the left, however, professional workers are seen as functionaries of government, exercising social control through the repressive state apparatus and creating a stigmatized and dependent welfare clientele. These critiques have, as Levitas (1986) puts it, been 'hi-jacked' by the new right in their attack on the welfare state, as the monopoly controls of professionals have been seen to provide a 'ratchet' effect for the expansion of state welfare programmes and state spending which operates only in the private interests of the welfare providers (see Chapter 7).

A second and alternative interpretation of the expansion of

professional workers pays attention to their emergence in the twentieth century under different structural conditions of labour markets and capitalist social relations from that which characterized the professions of the nineteenth century. Thus the shift from the self-employment of professionals under conditions of liberal market capitalism to employment in bureaucratic organizations is held to subject the newer professions to constraints of managerial priorities and authority which undermine their ability to be autonomous. This approach sees professional workers as subject to a formal subordination under private or state management by virtue of the fact that they sell their labour power, even though some employees may be privileged by special labour markets (Larson 1980). With respect to those employees that remain technically dominant, Larson notes that even 'they do not control key financial decisions and their own organizational authority is only delegated' (1980, p. 140).

To what extent then can the parallel with industrial workers be taken further? Are professional workers experiencing a proletarianization similar to that of craft workers in the nineteenth century, that is, is their work now becoming more routinized, fragmented and mechanized or to what extent has the labour market value of their skills and qualifications being devalued? Writers such as Oppenheimer (1973) and McKinley and Arches (1985) have argued that the spread of bureaucratic control has led to the proletarianization of professionals. Bureaucracy creates highly developed divisions of labour with associated fragmentation and narrow specialism as well as rules, standardized procedures and performance monitoring, which control the goals and work practices of professionals. McKinley and Arches also stress bureaucratization through the introduction of forms of management rationality characteristic of private industry, and the corporatization of health and welfare in the USA (see Chapter 7), which subverts medical practice to organizational goals such as profit or cost containment.

It can be argued though that professional labour still maintains an unusual degree of skill and discretion in carrying out specialized procedures and, as we discussed above, the ability to determine clients' needs and treatments and a role of policy determination. This has been recognized by labour process writers who have shown how management have devised alternative structures of control to harness the creative potential and initiative of higher-level workers, for example, Friedman's 'responsible autonomy' as a technique of control.

Larson (1980) also agrees that professional labour retains considerable degrees of technical control although she considers that they are nevertheless increasingly subject to management controls. Larson argues that under principles of cost-efficient productivity state and private managers attempt to produce a 'professional intensive' labour force. At the level of the labour process she finds evidence of the intensification and routinization of professional work. Pressures on the labour process however, are aggravated by adverse labour market conditions, in some cases creating a surplus population of specialists, which makes professional workers more dependent on their employers and less able to resist their authority.

Derber (1982) has argued that a minimum definition of proletarianization would include a shift from self-employment to dependent employment in which professionals' work also becomes effectively subject to management control. He distinguishes between ideological and technical proletarianization: 'The former involves the worker's loss of control over decisions concerning the goals, objectives and policy directions of his or her work. The latter represents the loss of control over decisions concerning how the technical tasks and procedures are to be carried out' (p.18). Derber argues that professional workers are subject to managerial control of a different type to that experienced by industrial workers. That is, professional workers experience subordination in their inability to define the ends and social purposes to which their work is put. Some professional workers, he argues, have been ideologically incorporated into their employing organization, identifying with management objectives and policies. In social work, for example, the case work orientation directed attention towards individual therapeutic rehabilitation rather than social or political concerns. Derber claims that 'Keeping social workers' focus on individual pathology and away from social oppression was of major importance to state agencies

. . . and formed the basis for a highly sophisticated ideological co-option, where social workers' moral concerns for the well-being of their clients could be accommodated in a form of practice that served institutional ends' (1983, p.333).

In return for ideological co-option professional workers, Derber argues, are able to preserve their technical autonomy. As long as professional workers identify with the objectives of senior management their continuing technical autonomy may serve management's interests more than it threatens them, diminishing the need for the rationalized methods of work control to which lower-level workers are subject.

Given, then, high levels of work autonomy and the ability to exercise initiative, expertise and judgement, some professional workers, it is claimed, will discharge their duties in ways consistent with senior management's aims. As Fox (1974) has described it, their employment relation is regulated by elements of high trust. According to Boreham (1983), the commitment and reliability of professional workers is also secured through extra-organizational sources of professional socialization and training, giving these workers a 'highly congenial organizational attitude'. However, as we discuss later in this chapter, the more powerful and prestigious professions have been able to exercise an important influence in the determination of social policy and remain the primary decision makers in the delivery of welfare services. It is because of this that state managers have continuously sought new forms of control as a discipline on professional providers (see for example Chapter 8). Before discussing the relation between the state and professional provider groups though, we first examine why some professional groups have been more successful than others in resisting managerial encroachments to their authority and autonomy.

OCCUPATIONAL CONTROL STRATEGIES

Several theorists of the professions have noted how the image of the free or independent professional established during specific historical conditions of the nineteenth century now operates not only as an ideological model for the newer and aspiring professions but also for those who have written about them. Historically the older classic professions such as law and medicine established a monopoly of control over recruitment, education, certification, and the content and conditions of their work. These practitioners were able to claim freedom from lay or external authority, the privilege of colleague evaluation and the practice of skills based on knowledge and training without supervision. Approaches to the study of the professions, however, have accepted the claims of the professionals at face value. Thus earlier conceptions of a profession argued that it was a special type of occupation which embodied essential qualities or 'traits', and occupations were assumed to fall along a continuum according to the number of traits that by various mechanisms they had acquired (for example see Millerson 1964, Greenwood 1957).[3]

Johnson (1972) in his critique of the trait approach has argued that professionalism must instead be seen as an historically specific form of occupational control. 'A profession is not then an occupation, but a means of controlling an occupation' (p.45). The purpose of such occupational control is self-government, and with state support legal monopoly over recruitment, training and certification. Such conditions, as Larson has argued, lead to the creation and maintenance of a protected or institutional market for professional services and a 'project of collective occupational and social ascension' (1980, p.141).

Occupational control strategies have been most usefully conceptualized as a process of social closure. Max Weber defined social closure as a 'process by which social collectivities seek to maximise rewards by restricting access to resources and opportunities to a limited circle of eligibles' (quoted in Parkin 1979, p.44). Parkin has been influential in recasting Weber's concept of social closure into two forms: that is, social closure as exclusion and social closure as usurpation. 'The distinguishing feature of exclusionary closure is the attempt by one group to secure for itself a privileged position at the expense of some other group through a process of subordination'. Usurpation on the other hand is a process of closure adopted by the excluded themselves as a direct response to their status as outsiders. For

Parkin, professionalization is a form of exclusionary social closure which relies on credentialism—the use of educational qualifications—'as a means of monitoring the entry to key positions in the division of labour' (1979, p.54).

Larson too has analysed the way in which education and the university in particular played a key role in the emergence of the classic older professions. The university provided a 'standardized and uniform system for training of professional procedures. It unified both the production of knowledge and the production of the professional producers'. The aim of professionalizing movements, Larson claims, was to 'make such a system of training the mandatory point of entry into professional practice, the monopolistic source of legitimate professional practice' (1980, p.142). Monopoly was however, justified by reference to universalistic and objective criteria of recruitment and achievement thereby masking the exclusion of certain categories of ineligibles such as women and less well-educated lower-class males. These strategies of social closure have enabled some occupational groups to achieve upward collective mobility and as a consequence have contributed to the structuring of social inequalities and, as we discuss below, the structuring of the division of labour, leading in the twentieth century to the formation of privileged but propertyless, intermediate or middle-class groups.

Professionalism as a form of social closure has therefore been an important strategy pursued by some occupational groups in order to obtain a privileged place within the division of labour. As Kreckel points out, though, whilst discussions of social closure have been important in understanding how occupational inequalities in the labour market are maintained, they 'have not so far been able to provide a systematic analysis of why certain groups within the labour sector of the labour market are in a better position to make successful use of strategies of closure than others' (1980, p.531).[4] Another way of putting this would be to ask why some occupational groups which pursue strategies of social closure become exposed to routinization and fragmentation of their work tasks and subordination to managerial authority, that is, the proletarianization of professional work described in Section 1 above, whilst other occupations are able to resist such encroachments on their autonomy.

One answer to this lies in the distinction made by Jamous and Peloille (1970) between the technicality and indetermination components of professional knowledge. Technicality refers to the extent to which a systematic body of knowledge is utilized in the justification of competence or expertise by occupations; it is the set of rules, procedures and solutions which are transferred to each generation of experts and learnt; as the authors put it, it is the part played in the production process by 'means that can be mastered and communicated in the form of rules' (p.112). The extent to which an occupation has a body of systematic knowledge, however, exposes it to codification and organizational regulation and control. Indeterminacy on the other hand refers to aspects of uncertainty in occupational knowledge, that is, the bases of an occupation's mystique, ideology, or sources of legitimation, for instance non-transferable or esoteric skills such as personal or advocacy skills, or 'bedside manner'.

Jamous and Peliolle claim that professions are occupations which have a high indetermination/technicality ratio. Those professions that successfully project a high degree of indeterminacy will be less susceptible to managerial or bureaucratic intervention and able to retain or create privileges which include a measure of work autonomy. Larson shows for example, how 'the secrecy and mystery which surround the creative process [of expert intellectual work] maximise the self governance conceded to experts'. In particular they are protected from the 'tyranny of the clock'; 'even if their products and organization of their work lives escape their control they are *masters of their time*' (1977, p.235).

Portwood and Fielding also show how privileges stem from vestiges of structures and ideologies of earlier and pre-industrial periods, in Britain, for example, norms of tradition and the status of a gentleman are still important claims to privilege in the established professions which, as the authors argue, gives them considerable protection from 'arbitrary or even rational control' (1981, p.766). Although the authors do not state it, the importance of the status of a gentleman of independent means for the professions also provided a method of excluding women from the nineteenth-century professions.

The aspiring professions are engaged in a project to protect and upgrade their work and labour-market conditions and have often resorted to the ideology of the established professions that emerged in the nineteenth century. They are however caught in a dilemma, for in their project they have to establish a systematic body of knowledge and practice skills which function as the basis for accreditation and legitimation of expertise. In so doing, though, they expose themselves to encroachments by managerial or bureaucratic controls. In social work for example, case work theory was an important symbol of social work's claim to professional status and provided a means of projecting a unified ideology amongst a fragmented occupation. 'In line with this thinking generic training was urged' (Parrys 1979, p.40). In Britain the creation of Social Service Departments after the Seebohm Report in 1968 has been considered to be a success for the social work elite, since the report affirmed the claims of social work to professionalism, establishing the generic social work role and generic training. But the actual implementation of SSDs involved the establishment of bureaucratic and managerial structures which incorporated attempts to define and break down the social workers' tasks in ways which aid the management and supervision of their work.

SEXUAL DIVISIONS OF LABOUR AND THE PROFESSIONS

The concept of occupational closure is important for our understanding of the divisions within the professional labour force and the social processes that have shaped them. However, the division of labour is not only technical, or even primarily technical, for tasks are also constructed and defined in gendered ways so that there is sexual division of labour between the established and semi-professions. As a consequence the semi-professions in the twentieth century are staffed mainly by women but are managed mainly by men, and serve the established and male professions (Hearn 1982).

Yet as Hearn notes, and this discussion so far has shown, the significance of sexual divisions of labour in the professions has received almost no attention in the mainstream literature. As in the labour process literature this input has had to come, with a few exceptions, from feminist writers.

A number of writers have documented the ways in which sexual divisions of labour have developed historically through patriarchal strategies of control and closure by the established and male-dominated professions, for example work on women and medicine (Ehrenreich and English 1979), on nursing (Gamarnikow 1978, Carpenter 1976), teaching (Parrys 1974) and in social work (Parrys 1979). Often these strategies involved attempts to exclude women from the institutional means of gaining qualifications: in medicine male practitioners prevented women from gaining access to qualifications for medical practice (Witz 1984), in teaching women were also initially excluded from universities and the ministry, and their education concentrated in colleges of education which emphasized training for elementary schools (Parrys 1974).

In addition ideological distinctions between masculine and feminine work have also been important in shaping the type of work carried out by the semi-professions. The work of the semi-professions mirrors the work performed by women in the home: caring, nurturing, and the handling of emotions. The divisions between the semi-professions and the established professions are therefore based on different 'spheres of competences' related to the sexual division of labour in the home. Gamarnikow for example has shown how nursing arose in the nineteenth century within a medical division of labour already dominated by doctors, all of whom were men. Nursing was created and defined as an independent occupational structure which in no way posed a threat to medical authority, since it emphasized the interconnections between 'femininity, motherhood, housekeeping and nursing'. Nursing was defined as women's work, and to be a good nurse one had to have the qualities of a 'good' woman. For Florence Nightingale this meant 'quietness, gentleness, patience, endurance, forbearance and obedience'—qualities which were to be used by nurses as 'helpers' in carrying out doctors' orders (Gamarnikow 1978, p.115-16).

Professionalizing strategies of the semi-professions have also, as we argue below, shaped the divisions of labour within the occupation, as occupational elites have sought to exclude the unqualified and untrained. Hearn (1982) notes that social work, teaching and nursing have provided middle- and upper-class qualified women with jobs of considerable authority over lower-class and unqualified women, thus introducing a divisive class element within the same occupation. Attempts to professionalize have also led to the development of professional codes, rules and procedures (the technicality component) which Hearn has argued has had the effect of 'masculinizing . . . the behaviour of practitioners' and makes it easier for men to enter the semi-professions. Once men enter the occupation they enter in highly discriminating ways that make a full-time career out of the profession, achieving the higher and more prestigious ranks and specializations.

PROFESSIONS AND THE STATE

Crucial to the development of professional strategies of social closure and the achievement of privileges has been the relationship of the professionals to the state. Johnson (1972) was one of the first to analyse the role of the state in relation to professions, when in formulating a typology of occupational control he argued that three types of control could be discerned: collegiate, patronage and mediation.[5] Important here are forms of state mediation where the state intervenes in the relationship between producer and customer to define both the needs of customers and the manner in which they will be met; the state guarantees a clientele and therefore work for the producers, and the resources for treatment. Under state mediation various occupations are increasingly incorporated into the organizational framework of government agencies, although these take different forms which are a result of the prior historical development of the occupation.

In later works Johnson (1977, 1980) related these three forms of control to the reproduction of the class structure, in particular the way in which professional occupations are

implicated in the appropriation of surplus value, in the realization of surplus value or, as in the case of welfare professionals, in the reproduction of labour power. Although
Johnson notes that there are variations in the extent to which
official or occupational definitions of clients' needs and treatments are dominant, these variations coincide with the requirements of capital in the reproduction process. He argues
that to the extent that occupational definitions fulfil the ideological and control functions of capital in the reproduction
process, then the profession is able to sustain its claims to
privilege and power. By reference to the concept of indetermination, discussed in the previous section, Johnson argues
that 'The strength of the ideological symbols which underpin
occupational power and privilege is directly related to the
extent to which the occupation fulfils the "global" functions of
capital in the reproduction process or merely applies such
definitions as a more or less routine labour process' (1980,
p.364).

Johnson recognizes, however, that welfare professions may
be relatively autonomous from the determining process of
appropriation of surplus value, that is, their political and
ideological practices may not be directly reducible to or
deducible from the relations of production. He sees these
professions as beneficiaries and not simply mechanisms of
reproduction of the class structure. In this way he notes the
tensions which are generated when the state attempts to
remove from occupational control those functions central to
the reproduction of capital, which set in train a process of
proletarianization. As we noted in the discussion of indetermination, 'professionalism' as an ideology is likely to become
more strident in the defensive action mounted by the occupation.

There are problems with Johnson's formulation however.
For example, he says little about the control processes which
are the result of intra-professional negotiations and conflicts,
or the processes which lead to the self-stratification of an
occupation (although in his earlier work he does describe the
ways in which state mediation has the effect of creating
divergent interests and orientations within an occupational
community, as for example between local and cosmopolitan

orientations). A further difficulty concerns his conception of the function of the state as only serving the reproduction of labour power or in some cases the appropriation and realization functions. Welfare provision was not developed entirely at the instigation of the dominant class but was also the product of struggles between the labour movement, the state and the dominant class. As we noted in Chapter 3, state welfare work is ambiguous and contradictory, it both reproduces healthy and educated labour power, and provides services which are a material resource for labour. As Gough (1979) expresses it, the welfare state exhibits both 'positive and negative' features; it is simultaneously a mechanism of repressive social control and enhances the social welfare and powers of individuals. An alternative formulation needs to take account of the ways in which the state both has to respond to the requirements of capital in its provision of welfare and has to provide welfare services which are circumscribed by public policy making and parliamentary and electoral acceptance.

The relationship of professionals to the state can perhaps be conceptualized more adequately by reference to notions of corporatism in which, as functional groups, professional provider groups are drawn into a specific relationship with the state in order to formulate and implement public policies. Corporatism has been seen as both a mode of state intervention and a mode of interest representation which has developed alongside parliamentary representative systems (Jessop 1979). Certain interest groups, for example bodies representing employers' associations or trade unions, have developed a degree of independent power which arises from their structural location in the division of labour. These 'functional' groups take part in regular negotiations with state agencies and develop a 'mutually dependent bargaining relationship in which favourable policy outcomes are traded for co-operation and expertise' (Cawson 1982, p.39). These groups not only represent their demands to state agencies but are also involved in the implementation of state policies.

Corporatist tendencies in late capitalist countries have usually been discussed in terms of tripartite structures of co-operation between the state, employers' associations and trade unions which have in recent decades attempted to establish a consensus with respect to incomes policies, prices and industrial relations. As such, tripartism has been seen as a mode of policy making in which the government can attempt to promote conditions of profitable accumulation as 'the co-operation of the corporate is required which commits them to the overall legitimacy of the existing economic system' (Jessop 1979). Moreover corporatism is a form of class domination, since the unions must ensure that they restrain and effectively control the behaviour of the rank and file. In Britain however, the tripartite structures of the mid-1970s have not been seen as a fully corporatist system in which 'union leaders accept the priorities determined by government and employers and then impose the required restraint on their members' but as a form of 'bargained' corporatism in which union leaders 'press for major concessions in exchange for the restraint they will offer' (Crouch 1979, p.131).

These corporatist tendencies in Britain in the 1970s proved unstable and contributed to the growing industrial unrest of that period, and since 1979 the Conservative government has made no attempt to gain union co-operation at a national level. But, as Cawson notes, 'to dismiss the significance of corporatism because of the instability of one of its forms— tripartism— is to overlook the much more firmly embedded structures of corporate representation in a far wider area of social policy making' (p.41). Cawson argues that it is in the area of social policy determination and its implementation that 'corporate alliances' between the professional provider groups and state agencies have developed.

In Chapter 3 it was argued that the relationship between the state and professional groups is one in which the state selectively favours the interests of certain groups over those of others. Thus those groups who are able to make the most effective contribution to the avoidance of risks, for example fractions of capital, organized labour and professional elites, are granted 'structurally determined privileges'. 'The state selectively intervenes so that these groups are able to define the scope of "realistic" issues and demands, which are then filtered through political and administrative processes'. The state not only turns to certain groups for the formulation of policies but also for their implementation.

Not all social policy decisions are made through corporatist arrangements. As Cawson noted, Offe's analysis of the allocative and productive activities of the state provides a useful means of analysing the relationship between the state and professional provider groups in the state welfare sector. For example, whilst allocative policy (that is, social security benefits, or taxation) is most effectively administered through a bureaucratic and rational legal organization, 'the production of welfare services involves the collaboration of professional providers in the determination of goals' (Cawson 1982, p.56).

It was suggested that state administrators lacked clear criteria on which to make decisions regarding the provision of welfare services, and have therefore depended on the judgement of professional providers as to what are adequate resources and types of treatment. Not only has this meant that professional provider groups have had an expansionary impact on budgets, but also that the interests of the more powerful professions have been privileged. This mutual compliance and dependence between the state and the professional groups has been important in the determination and implementation of social policy. Cawson suggests that the NHS and the monopoly controls of the medical profession are probably the most corporatist in the field of social policy (for a different interpretation see Mercer 1984), but elements of corporatism can also be found in education, town planning and to a lesser extent in the personal social services.

Corporatism, however, is only one of a number of strategies the state may follow. The Conservative government in the 1980s, for example, has pursued authoritarian and repressive policies and in the economic sphere, as Goldthorpe has argued (1985), strategies are evident which seek to create or expand the areas in which workers are exposed to the effects of market forces and to the exercise of employers' prerogatives. In social policy too, as we describe in other sections of this book, the state has been concerned to implement more bureaucratic and centralized forms of control and more recently various forms of market rationality.

Nevertheless, in terms of our concern with the structuring

of work within welfare organizations, it can be suggested that the mutual dependence and compliance between the state and certain professional groups has led, at certain historical conjunctures, to divisions of labour within the state work-force. The granting of special privileges to some professional occupations involves them in attempts to maintain these privileges by engaging in strategies of solidarism and exclusion of other occupational groups, of horizontal demarcation between occupational groups or types of qualifications, and strategies which involve patriarchal forms of control (Kreckel 1980, Hearn 1982). The consequent subordination of other occupational groups has meant that they too have pursued professionalizing strategies by seeking state sponsorship, which in turn has contributed to the self-stratification of many professional occupations. That is, divisions within the occupation between the trained and untrained, qualified and unqualified and between professionalism and unionism. These processes are discussed in more detail below by reference to the NHS and the professionalizing strategies of health occupations.[5]

PROFESSIONAL OCCUPATIONS IN THE NHS

Occupations pursuing professionalizing strategies have sought the co-operation and legal backing of the state in their attempts to gain a monopoly over areas of knowledge, recruitment and training. Historically some occupations have been able to achieve a monopoly before the intervention of the state into the provision of social or welfare services. The medical profession, for example, achieved a monopoly position during a period when state machinery for regulating and controlling medicine was weak (Parrys 1977). By the end of the nineteenth century nursing reforms were incorporated and subordinated in a technical and sexual division of medical labour dominated by doctors. Ideological claims of responsibility for the patient and authority in the diagnostic relationship have further ensured that emergent allied health occupations have developed under the control and direction of medical practitioners.

Medical hegemony was ratified by the privileged position the profession retained after the negotiations which created the NHS. Here the BMA was able to achieve favourable terms and conditions of employment, a crucial role in policy determination, the right to define and take medical decisions and an acknowledgement that 'health auxiliaries must remain under the supervision and tutelage of the general medical profession' (Bevan, quoted in Armstrong 1976). More recently though, medical hegemony has been challenged by the reorganization of administrative structures (there have been four such reorganizations in the past twenty years), designed to shift power away from the doctors. Additionally, there have been increased pressures on the medical profession from the paramedics (reflecting changes in health policy and technology) and from the development of trade unionism in the 1970s.

Vulnerable to both medical and managerial control, nurses too have also pursued strategies of professional control and closure. By seeking state sponsorship in their professional aspirations, however, nursing elites have contributed to the self-stratification of the nursing work process and labour markets. In their attempts to resist the intrusion of untrained labour, nursing elites created a hierarchical 'grade system' of trained and untrained nurses with corresponding opportunities for promotion. Yet nurses as a profession have never been able to gain control of recruitment, which the state in its use of the power to license practice, has retained, 'keeping open a plentiful supply of cheap labour' (Bellaby and Oribabor 1980). As Doyal shows, one of the sources of cheap labour were women from overseas who 'provided both a supply of extremely cheap labour whilst in training, as well as a permanent reserve of skilled workers' (Doyal *et al.* 1981, p.64 see also Ch. 4). The nursing workforce has thus developed a highly differentiated division of labour, stratified along class and ethnic lines, and part of an overall gendered division of medical labour.

In the 1960s, with the implementation of the Salmon Report, nursing elites were also instrumental in the co-option of nursing structures into management, further weakening the links between nursing grades, and dividing nurses into those orientated to management and those committed to clinical nursing. The Salmon Report was part of attempts by the state in the 1960s to increase labour productivity in the public services, directing scientific management techniques to the largest occupational groups, nurses and ancillary workers. The application of a 'foreign' rationality to nursing structures created however the preconditions for increased trade-union membership and organization (the effects on trade unionism of ancillary workers is discussed in Chapter 6). For nurses, the implementation of the Salmon Report imposed hierarchic, bureaucratic controls on nursing structures. Nursing work was further divided by the hiving off of management roles above ward level and the removal of unskilled work to auxiliary workers, leaving ward-level staff with a loss of control over previous work practices. Imposed on the pre-existing 'grade system', this bureaucratization of work reinforced the sense of disillusionment experienced by many of the rank and file workers towards the lack of promotion opportunities, pay and conditions of work and exclusion from elitist professional associations (Carpenter 1976).

These conditions proved fertile ground for the development of trade unionism amongst nurses in the 1970s, contributing, as we argue in Chapter 6, to the increasing militancy of health workers during that period and subsequent government responses to weaken the public sector unions. More recently too the government has implemented new management structures which have restructured nursing work and, as we discuss in Chapter 8, the highly stratified divisions of labour in nursing, as well as divisions between unionism and professionalism, have left nurses vulnerable and with little ability to resist these new policies.

CONCLUSION

Focusing on welfare professionals, it has been argued that in the state sector the mutual dependence and compliance between the state and professional provider groups has privileged certain professional occupations. Privileges bestowed by employers secure for the professional group organizational positions of authority, and control and autonomy in their work in the exercise of initiative, expertise and judgement. These professional groups retain an important role in policy determination, and in the decision making hierarchy of the organization. Other professional or semi-professional groups, however, may have little say in the purposes of their work and may discharge their duties in ways that are more consistent with senior management's objectives. Although for these workers, as Derber (1983) has argued, there may be no necessity for coercive or Taylorist forms of control since the goals and objectives of the professional workers have been subverted to those of the organization.

The higher-level professions will themselves attempt to maintain their privileges by engaging in strategies of solidarism and exclusion of other occupational groups, of horizontal demarcation between occupational groups or types of qualifications (Kreckel 1980), and in strategies which involve patriarchal forms of control (Hearn 1982). Some of these strategies, as we have seen, emphasize the indeterminacy of the occupation, the uniqueness and exclusiveness of professional knowledge and practice, Larson has further argued that the ideology of professionalism, especially the emphasis on individualism and status, prevents alliances with other workers. 'The concern with status . . . works as a preventive against the unity—and the unionization—of professional workers themselves' (1977, p.236).

The effect of these professional strategies and ideologies is to weaken the bargaining position of other occupational groups within the labour force and to shape and reinforce both the technical and sexual divisions of labour. The subordinate professions have themselves engaged in professionalizing strategies in conjunction with the state, which have led to the self-stratification of occupations along both class and gendered lines, and created divisions between qualified and unqualified and between professionalism and unionism. Professionalizing strategies have also often involved attempts to increase the technical component of professionalism, that is, the systematic body of rules and procedures which exposes them to greater management controls. Appeals to the ideology or indeterminancy of professionalism may then

'represent an attempt at a last-ditch defence against subordination' (Larson 1977, p.219). However as Larson says 'as long
as the protests of subordinate professional workers ask for
more of these individual privileges [of the higher-level profes-
sionals], as long as that is the main purpose of their corporate
associations, their potential disloyalty can be easily managed'
(p.237).

NOTES

1. Two different interpretations of the class location of educated labour
   or middle-class occupations are as follows: (i) professional occupations together with managerial, administrative and scientific
   occupations have been perceived as emerging as a separate and identifiable class which does not fit easily into the dual model of bourgeoisie
   and proletariat, for example, in Britain, Goldthorpe (1982) has developed the concept of the service class, and in America the Ehrenreichs
   (1979) have put forward the notion of a 'professional managerial
   class'; (ii) other writers from within the Marxist perspective have
   attempted to incorporate the growth of professional and other highly-
   educated labour within theoretical schemes of the class structure, for
   example, the 'new working class' theories of Mallet (1975), theories of
   productive and non-productive labour put forward by writers such as
   Poulantzas (1975) and Carchedi (1977), and Wright's (1976, 1985)
   view of the contradictory location of educated labour within class
   relations.
2. There is an extensive literature, but on health see Doyal (1983),
   Roberts (1981), and Ehrenreich and English (1979); on social work
   see Dale and Foster (1986).
3. Millerson (1964) for example distilled from the sociological literature
   twenty-three elements or traits which had been included in definitions
   of a profession by twenty-one different authors. Millerson concluded
   that the most frequently mentioned traits were (i) skills based on
   theoretical knowledge, (ii) the provision of training and education,
   (iii) testing the competence of members (iv) a professional association
   (v) a professional code of conduct (vi) altruistic service.
3. Kreckel attempts to do this by extending Parkins' concepts of exclusion and solidarism into a fivefold classification 'of social
   mechanisms affecting bargaining strength [of workers] in advanced
   capitalist labour markets', these are, (i) demarcation, (ii) exclusion,
   (iii) solidarism, (iv) inclusion, and (v) exposure (1980, p.541). These
   mechanisms are applied only to the private employment sector,
   although Witz (1984) has used the analytical framework of Kreckel to
   examine patriarchal strategies of control in medical occupations.

4. Collegiate control, in which the professional group defines the needs of the consumer and the manner in which these needs are met, for example, medical practitioners and lawyers; second, forms of patronage, where the customer defines his or her own needs and the manner in which they shall be met: one example here is accountants who serve the interests of corporate organizations; and third, various forms of mediative control where a third party defines both the needs and the manner in which they will be met: state mediation is important here as it has intervened in the relationship between producer and customer to define for example clients' welfare needs, a guaranteed clientele, and the resources available (Johnson 1972).

5. Evidence of this self-stratification can also be seen in teaching. The Parrys, in describing the failure of the teachers' registration movement from the nineteenth century onwards, have said: 'divisions within teaching, themselves based in class and religion, as well as in sexual divisions have been important in preventing the emergence of a unified and self governing profession. The opposition of established middle class groups to the assimilation of the elementary teacher was historically crucial. In the event these forces were crystallised in the policies of governments and in their record of educational legislation. The stark fact now is that the state having become the most powerful force in education has a vested interest in opposing the ideal of the teachers' registration movement, that is blocking the establishment of a self governing profession' (Parry and Parry 1974, p.69).

6 The Political Economy of Public Service Unionism

In the post-war period the nature and timing of the development of public sector unionism in the UK and US show a number of similarities, including their implication in the fiscal crisis of the state, and subsequent government responses. These similarities are remarkable in view of the well-documented differences between the American and British labour movements, and of the 'exceptional' features of American private sector unions. This chapter examines the political economic context within which public sector unions in the two countries have developed in the post-war period. Whilst there has been a recent interest in Anglo-American comparisons of labour relations from this perspective[1] (for example Edwards 1981, 1983a, Shalev 1981, Kassalow 1977), these discussions have concentrated on the declining private sector unions and there has been little consideration, with the exception of institutional accounts, of the growing public unionism.

The following discussion uses the analytical framework of the sector model developed by O'Connor and the critical theorists, which differentiates the economy into private and public production sectors[2] (O'Connor 1973, Habermas 1976, Offe 1976). Using this model it is possible to distinguish the different modes of rationality governing each sector, 'the different modes of productivity, levels of worker bargaining power and levels of overtly political determination of wage levels' (Dunleavy 1980a, p.382). This interpretation of the growth and militancy of unionism amongst state service workers in the post-war period is therefore as an aspect of their structural location within a sector which is governed by a non-market rationality, yet dependent on the profitability and prosperity of the private sector.

Despite similarities in the timing and nature of their development the public sector unions in the US and the UK also show differences which reflect, as in the private sector unions, the different historical development of labour relations, the particular patterns of class action and mobilization, the role of the state, and the influence of institutional arrangements in the two countries. The first section of this chapter therefore discusses the historical developments of unions in the US and UK and considers the theoretical propositions of O'Connor and other writers with regard to the different sectors of production in advanced capitalist countries and their implications for labour relations. Section two compares the growth and militancy of public sector unions in the two countries, and section three examines the role of these unions in the fiscal crises of the states in the US and UK. Section four examines the empirical evidence that is now beginning to emerge on labour relations in the recession of the 1980s, although there is as yet limited evidence on public sector unionism.[3]

THE DEVELOPMENT OF LABOUR RELATIONS IN THE UK AND THE USA

The distinctive features of United States unionism, namely, the absence of a politically organized labour movement, the low density and narrow base of unionism and the emphasis on workplace conflict and job control, have been explained in terms of the historical conditions prior to and during industrialization. Thus, the absence of a feudal past, the successive waves of immigrants resulting in 'hierarchies and antagonisms amongst ethnic and religious groups', the presence of an open frontier, early white male suffrage, and an ideology of individualism have all been held to prohibit the formation of a strong and widespread labour movement and the lack of class consciousness amongst the American working class (Edwards 1981, Gordon *et al.* 1982, Kassalow 1969).

Littler (1982) has shown too how the different forms of labour relations between the UK and US reflect the timing and pattern of the establishment of industrial capitalism and in particular the transition from competitive to monopoly capitalism. Widespread unionism in Britain was established prior to the rise of large corporations and the introduction of Taylorism and systematic management. For the first two decades of this century firms in Britain were predominantly under familial or entrepreneurial ownership, and although employers did attempt to remove craft forms of control over the production process, workers were able to resist and maintain some autonomy. Moreover, the relative lateness of the emergence of large corporations in the 1920s and 1930s also entailed a weaker application of scientific management and rationalized control systems. Trade-union resistance to management controls, especially amongst craft workers, has meant that such groups have enjoyed more influence over the labour process, and for longer periods, than elsewhere.

In the US large monopoly corporations emerged two decades before Britain, and rationalized systematic management was established much earlier, more rapidly and before the unions were able to organize a large proportion of the work force. By the time the unskilled groups in America were unionized they faced 'solidified patterns of work organization' and the successful wresting of management control away from the skilled workers. Although craft unions in the US and the UK in the nineteenth century were broadly similar, Edwards (1983a) has argued that a decisive influence in their later development was the intensity of American employers' hostility to unions and their readiness to take action to remove craft union constraints over the operations and challenges to their authority. Employers were then able to exploit ethnic and religous divisions and the values of individualism within the American working class. It is in this context that 'business unionism' was shaped, as unions were forced into a defensive posture.

The intensity of employer opposition and the intervention of the state during the New Deal era shaped the later developments in American unionism, especially the emergence of contract unionism and removal of autonomous shop-floor action. After the establishment of collective bargaining in the 1930s the unions in the immediate post-war period found that low unemployment and the beginnings of an economic boom gave them a strong bargaining position. The high incidence of strikes during this period rekindled government and employer hostility, leading eventually to the Taft Hartly Act which curtailed union rights, but established a capital-labour accord with a set of arrangements for regulating labour relations; for example, union recognition, grievance procedures and seniority rules for promotions and lay-offs.

The climate of hostility influenced the unions' pursuit of economistic aims for high wages, working conditions and welfare funding together with an acceptance of 'contractual responsibility', the formal procedures of collective bargaining. In so doing, Brody says, 'they subverted a claim to participation in matters of management' (1981). Management was therefore able to increase its control over redundancies, increase productivity, and reorganize the labour process.

Since then workers in the strongly unionized sector have made considerable gains in terms of higher wages and private welfare funding. The large monopoly corporations have been able to make these concessions to labour by passing on price increases or by generating higher levels of productivity. But the gains of workers in the monopoly sector have been made at the expense of those workers in the competitive and non-unionized sectors of the economy where employers can only survive by protecting their profit margins and resisting the setting up or the claims of unions.

In the US, then, the gap between the strongly unionized monopoly sector and the weakly unionized competitive sector is much more pronounced than it is elsewhere, and the gap has been widening each year since the mid-1950s, as the overall density of unionism has declined. The decline in American unionism is associated with the decline in manufacturing industries and the rise in service industries. Uneven economic development has meant the flight of capital from the unionized north-eastern states to either the Third World countries or the relatively union-free southern 'sunbelt' states of America. In the south, employers have used a variety of tactics to prevent workers from joining unions. Roy (1980) has described these tactics as 'fear stuff, sweet stuff and evil stuff', that is, inducing fear at the consequences of joining unions (fear stuff), the provision of benefits or improvements if they don't join a union (sweet stuff) or the presentation of the imagery of the evil forces of unionism (evil stuff). In the face of such opposition the business unions 'resting comfortably in the high wage sector of the economy' (Davis 1982) have abdicated attempts to organize low-waged workers in the service sector who are predominantly women or ethnic minority workers. As Davis has noted, the trade-union movement in the US has managed to organize only two million out of the thirty-two million new jobs which were created between 1960 and 1980 (1982).

These developments in the US have been discussed by O'Connor (1973) who has suggested that in the private monopoly sector wages are determined by quasi-political bargaining structures between the strongly organized trade unions and the corporations. The monopoly sector's structural position as a price maker, and the small share of its total costs accounted for by labour costs, enables it to grant union wage demands by passing on price increases, or by generating higher levels of productivity. In return for higher wages, union leaders abstain from resisting productivity rises, and by acting as the 'guarantors of management prerogatives' help to maintain labour discipline. As workers are expelled from the monopoly sector, since high wages encourage labour-saving devices and reorganizations of the labour process, they transfer to the competitive sector to seek employment. Competition in this sector, however, tends to keep wages low and discourage technical progress and increases in productivity. The state, too, tends to absorb the surplus labour or has to provide benefits and services for the unemployed or poor.

O'Connor's model, however, was developed with reference to the US, where the weakness of the labour movement, the small proportion of the labour force that is unionized, and the economistic aims of union leaders means that a decline of employment in the monopoly sector does follow from wage increases there. Hill (1981) has argued that in Britain the greater spread and strength of trade unionism has meant that, until recently, productivity gains did not necessarily follow wage increases and that unions were often able to resist redundancies and new techniques and controls. Nor is there the same gap between the unionized and non-unionized sectors of the economy, nor the degree of labour mobility between them that exists in the US. In Britain in the 1960s higher wages were therefore either passed on in higher prices or rose partly at the expense of capital; the consequences being inflation or a profits squeeze.

Glyn and Harrison's (1980) analysis of the condition of the economies of the advanced capitalist countries in the late 1960s shows that those economies were characterized by tight labour markets, rising money wages and international competition between firms, preventing them from passing on wage increases in prices. The result was a squeeze on the profits of companies. The reactions of governments in western Europe were, at different times, deflation and the use of incomes policies. Incomes policies can be most strictly imposed on public employees and, as discussed later, the deterioration in their pay levels compared to those of workers in the private corporate sector led, in many cases, to increased unionization and industrial militancy. Efforts by governments in the 1960s to involve employers and union leaders in the restraint of wage increases eventually alienated the rank and file of many unions, and a wave of strike protests took place throughout western Europe in the late 1960s, stimulated by the more general social unrest and protest of that period.

In Britain increased militancy was associated with the rise of shop-floor bargaining and wide variations between the earnings of workers in different plants and industries in the private manufacturing sector. Edwards has observed of this period that the 'rise in shop floor bargaining gave workers the organizational resources to engage in large numbers of strikes' (1983b). Associated with these strikes were 'pressures on workers' real wages through inflation, the characteristics of the tax system and the relatively low levels of unemployment'. The Donovan report claimed that this high level of strike activity was due to the two systems of industrial relations existing in Britain at that time, namely, the 'formal' and 'informal' systems. Since then, however, the 'informal' or workplace or plant-level system of bargaining in the private sector has increasingly been replaced by more formal procedures at the local level, the encouragement by management of the 'centralization, formalization and professionalization of shop stewards and their organizations' and a trend to their 'incorporation' within more bureaucratic forms of control (Terry 1983). The Donovan analysis could not, however, explain the nature of the large number of public sector strikes which occurred in the 1970s, and which were characterized by 'formal' or centralized systems of collective bargaining.

O'Connor, along with writers such as Habermas and Offe, claims that highly unionized labour in the monopoly sector has been 'bought off' in the advanced capitalist countries in the post-war period, as high wages and concessions are offered in return for loyalty and peace. These writers suggest that such 'political wages' tend to promote a 'class compromise', so that conflict, although still endemic, is partially immunized and displaced into other sectors of society. The locus of conflict changes from those directly implicated in conditions of exchange between capital and labour, to state employees or state clients who are external (but indirectly dependent on) the capital–wage labour nexus. The effects of this class compromise are given by Habermas as; (i) discrepancies between private and public sector wages and a sharpening of wage disputes as state workers seek comparability with private sector wages, (ii) inflation, which works to redistribute income to the disadvantage of the unorganized and marginal groups, (iii) a permanent crisis in government finances together with public poverty, and (iv) uneven regional and sectoral economic development (1976).

The state sector's labour-intensive nature, the ambiguities of calculating productivity increases, and the relatively low gains of productivity that are possible mean however that, for any given level of inflation, the costs of the state sector will rise relative to those of the private sector. The mechanisms of this relative cost effect are, according to O'Connor, exacerbated by increased wage levels as a result of militant actions on the part of state workers. In turn, rising relative costs of the state sector is one of the factors affecting the fiscal crisis of governments. Gough (1979) has usefully documented the other factors influencing the growth of state expenditure as: population changes; new and improved welfare services; and the growth of 'new social needs' as a result of the 'diswelfares' of economic progress. The result is the tendency for state expenditure to grow more rapidly than the means of financing it. For O'Connor the source of this fiscal crisis is the discrepancy between the growing socialization of costs and the continuing private appropriation of profits.

These theoretical propositions ignore, however, the importance of class conflict in explaining the growth of state welfare measures and the variations in working-class organization and action which have shaped the nature and extent of state-provided goods and services in different countries (Gough 1979). In addition the state itself has had an important influence in shaping organizational resources, including industrial relations structures, which allow the working class to mobilize its demands (Edwards 1983a) and therefore influence the forms and extent of public welfare that is provided. As Edwards argues, in the US the intervention of the state in industrial relations has helped to alter the character of workplace relations, and this has been significant for later organized industrial conflict. The activities of the state in the New Deal period were particularly important in shaping union rights and collective bargaining processes, which were then consolidated after the war in the manner described above, namely, the containment of industrial conflict within the workplace.

As we have seen, collective bargaining involved both wages and fringe and welfare benefits, so that the gains of union members were at the expense of those in the non-unionized competitive sector. The role of organized labour in the political system was defined as another 'interest group' rather than as a class-based activity (Navarro 1985). Consequently conflict with employers and demands for improvements in working-class life chances have remained in the workplace, at the industrial level, rather than being pursued through the political system (and hence the paradox that industrial conflict in America has persistently been at a higher level than in other advanced countries) (Shalev 1981, Edwards 1981, 1983a).

The lack of pressure from organized labour for social policy reforms meant that these were not implemented between the New Deal period and the 1960s when social unrest and riots in the cities, and pressure from the civil rights, welfare rights, students' and tenants' protest movements led to the 'Great Society' programmes; the urban aid and other programmes of the federal government. However, these welfare reforms never gained the widespread legitimacy of the welfare provisions in the UK and were to be more temporary and insecure, giving way to the right-wing 'single issue' protests of the 1970s. Recent evidence suggests that the Great Society programmes (those directed at the most vulnerable sections of the population) elicit less support than those social programmes established during the New Deal period which benefited the waged and salaried population (Navarro 1985).

In Britain, the more strongly organized labour movement, with a higher density of unionization amongst unskilled as well as skilled workers, a more unified union movement and strong links to a labour-based political party, has meant that conflict with capital has been pursued through the political sphere as well as in the workplace. Although World War II laid the groundwork for the welfare state as part of the 'settlement' between capital and labour, the second expansion of welfare services and improvements in the social wage came in the 1960s as a result of the increased 'economic and political leverage of the organized working class' (Gough 1979). The concern with the strength of rank and file workers and the 'disorder' of shop-floor labour relations led successive governments in the 1970s to intervene in regulating income levels and the previously voluntary industrial relations system. The intervention of the state in these areas, however, has had contradictory effects, one of which, as discussed in the next section, is the growth and militancy of public sector unions.

THE GROWTH AND MILITANCY OF PUBLIC SERVICE UNIONS

In the United States, public employment grew by eight million between 1952 and 1980, most of the growth occurring in the health and education services. However, because of population and labour market growth, public employment as a percentage of the total labour force has remained almost stable. In Britain, the largest expansion in public sector employment took place in the period immediately after World War II, so that the growth up to 1980 has been incremental, adding 1.7 million jobs, a quarter of the workforce. Nevertheless, public service employment represents the main employment growth in this period as both the private sector and nationalized industries have shed jobs. The growth has been greatest in the health services and local government. In both the US and the UK the expansion of the public service sector has been an important factor in the increase in women's employment and in the shift to part-time work (see Chapter 4).

In the United States union members as a proportion of all employees declined in the private sector from 31% in 1970, to 23% in 1980, to 19% in 1984, whilst in the public sector union membership has increased from 33% in 1970, to 36% in 1980 and remained at that level until 1984 (Cullen 1985). Through the federal urban aid programmes in the 1960s, the growth in public services has been greatest at the state and local government levels, so that public service unionism has increased most at this level. Public unionism has also made most progress in the north-eastern and upper mid-western cities where the concentration of labour and the influence of private sector unions provided a more favourable climate for unionization. In the southern and western states, employer hostility also applies to public sector unions. By 1980, according to the US Bureau of the Census, 48.8% of all state and local government employees belonged to labour organizations, although this ranged from 10% in Arkansas state to 77.6% in New York City (quoted in Kearney 1984).

Public service union membership in the United States increased after favourable legislation passed in the late 1950s gave trade union recognition and collective bargaining rights to federal employees and later to some state and local government employees, even though not all states have passed legislation providing for collective bargaining for public employees. Inflation and the high visibility of wage levels of private corporate sector workers, and a willingness to obtain some of the gains workers in that sector had made, seem also to have been important in influencing public service union growth and later industrial action. More recently union membership has grown as there has been an increase in the number of workers who are overeducated for their jobs, and an increase in the rationalization and intensification of work in the public services.

Many of the workers taken on in the public services were women who remained confined to lower-level, routinized work and lacked opportunities of promotion, and even where women gained work in the independent primary jobs they were subordinate to male professionals or managers. Although there was no special commitment to organizing women workers as women, but rather to organizing particular occupational groups which happened to be feminized, an unintended consequence has been that women in the 1970s and 1980s have become a significant part of public sector unionism and increasingly active participants (Bell 1985, Milkman 1985).

In Britain, unionization in the public sector has been higher than in the private sector throughout the post-war period, but whilst union organization has a long tradition in the nationalized industries, only in the 1970s was there a significant development in unionism in the public service sector. In the period 1969-1979, the health services, local government, and education services added 1.5 million union members, nearly 50% of total national union growth. Much of this growth is associated with increased white-collar and female unionization.

Prior to the 1970s, labour relations in the public services were depoliticized through the centralized Whitley system of collective bargaining, which enabled governments to keep tight control on pay levels, and insulated local management form workplace bargaining. The workforce was largely acquiescent, weakly unionized and orientated towards professionalism or a public service ethic. In the 1960s and 1970s the introduction of more bureaucratic forms of control in the public services, and state intervention to regulate incomes and industrial relations in the wider economy, transformed the nature of labour relations in the public service sector. A direct impetus to trade unionism came from the introduction of scientific management techniques to manual groups in local government and nurses and ancillary workers in the NHS. The introduction of bonus schemes for ancillary workers in the NHS, for example, brought groups of workers together for the first time and encouraged the emergence of shop stewards and local collective bargaining (Manson 1976). For nurses, the implementation of the Salmon Report in the 1960s imposed further divisions on top of the pre-existing grade system, and fostered the preconditions for increased trade-union membership and organization by creating a 'mass of workers whose career mobility as blocked' (Carpenter 1982; see also Chapter 5).

However, it was state intervention to regulate incomes and industrial relations during the 1960s and 1970s which had the most significant impact on work relations and trade unionism in the public service sector. By the late 1960s the cumulative effect of government incomes policies, inflation, and high wages amongst some key groups of private sector workers led to a sense of grievance and perceived discrimination on the part of public sector workers. The application of incomes policies during the period 1969-1974 was the direct cause of industrial action amongst several groups of public service workers, most of whom had never been on strike before. In turn industrial action increased union membership and local organization. Industrial relations legislation in the 1970s, although directed initially towards subverting the militancy of rank and file workers in the private sector, also encouraged shop-floor organization and the growth of shop-steward movements in the public services, encouraging trade-union consciousness, activity, and membership.

Thereafter the nature of management–labour relations changed. The vocational, public service ethic and obligation of loyalty on the workers' side became a more instrumental orientation with an emphasis on the cash nexus (recent management policies have exacerbated this trend—see Chapter 8). For some groups, for example ancillary workers in the NHS, the disputes raised issues of control which challenged government policy (Manson 1976) and other groups became more politicized as issues of pay, conditions of work and especially the content and purpose of their work involved them with the government more directly.

In the USA the increase in strike action in the public sector occurred after 1965 and reached a peak in 1979,[4] whereas in Britain strike action increased significantly in the early 1970s, and has continued throughout the 1980s. There are, however, considerable differences between the shape and character of strikes in the two countries, reflecting the differences in legislation and bargaining arrangements. In the United States, the highly decentralized nature of collective bargaining has meant that strikes amongst public employees are local events, (over 90% are at the local rather than state or federal levels) involve small groups of workers and are of shorter duration than those in Britain.[5] In most states legislation prohibits public employees from taking strike action (although in practice this does not prevent them), and the newness of union organization, lack of strike funds, and intense employer hostility also contribute to the pressure to settle disputes more quickly. In Britain, the opposite patterns prevails, where the centralized nature of collective bargaining means that strikes in the public sector 'tend to involve a relatively large number of workers, last a substantial length of time, and result in a high number of working days lost' (Beaumont 1982).[6]

THE FISCAL CRISIS OF THE UK AND USA STATES

In America the fiscal crisis has found its clearest expression at the local level of the urban cities. The fiscal crisis of New York City in 1975 is the most famous example but, although New York is in many respects unique since it maintains more public welfare services than other cities, many of the older cities, such as Cleveland, Chicago, Detroit, and San Francisco have also experienced similar financial difficulties and political conflicts. The urban fiscal crisis in these cities is associated with uneven economic development as the corporations have sought new locations in the southern and western states, with the cheaper land, lower wage rates and a more manipulable workforce. The population movements in response to these economic shifts leaves the lower income groups in the inner cities, with their greater demands for public services and less ability to pay. For example, between 1965 and 1972 New York

City lost 16% of its jobs, Philadelphia 17% and New Orleans nearly 20% (Tabb 1978).

Such economic decline erodes the tax base of the metropolis and intensifies demands of the low-income groups for public jobs and services. These cities were also the centre for the riots and protest movements of the 1960s, which later increased public expenditure and led to the metropolitan cities' dependence on revenues from state and federal budgets. In turn increased welfare aid attracted more low-income groups into the cities. The 1970s, however, saw a decline in intergovernmental aid but not in the demands placed on it, so that in New York city, for example, state and federal aid from 1965-1973 grew by an average of 50% per annum, but for 1973-1975 the growth rate was 8% (Tabb 1978). 'Rising expenditures and limited tax revenues forced cities into higher tax rates, greater short-term debt and an accelerating dependence on state and federal finance' (Friedland 1981, p.370).

In late 1974 the large banks in New York City sold their city securities, and in 1975 the market for the city's securities collapsed, leaving the state and federal governments to set up institutions to supervise the city's finances. These institutions were dominated by the city's financial and business elites, who negotiated a number of 'give backs' with the public unions, reducing the city's workforce by 20% as a result of lay-offs and job attrition, and freezing wages. The unions committed 40% of their pension funds to the city's bonds, which has since had the effect of moderating wage demands and strike threats.

Since the high local taxes fell most heavily on home owners, their tax protests, later to grow into a national movement, were directed to the most visible groups, the militant municipal unions and urban poor. Friedland has argued, however, that the sources of the fiscal crisis lay not simply in the demands of the public unions and the urban poor, but also in the capital expenditure programmes designed to finance projects which increase local profitable investment and, it was hoped, economic growth. Whilst the tax revolt was directed towards those most politically vulnerable, the poor and the municipal workers, 'the local organization of private investment remained unquestioned, un-touched and unruffled'

(Friedland 1981, p.371).[7]

In California, Proposition 13 made deep cuts in property taxes and set a permanent limit on future increases; it also signalled the wave of popular tax revolts across the United States[8]. In those states which have since imposed tax and expenditure limitations (twenty-three states by 1982), there have been large reductions in public jobs and services. Eight years later, however, the costs of measures to reduce public expenditure have been the impoverishment of public services and the deterioration of the physical and social infrastructure of the inner cities. The gap between the rich and poor has widened, and the decline in public schools and housing has particularly affected the poor, the homeless and recent immigrants.

In Britain the fiscal crisis was experienced in a different form to that in the States, at a national level rather than at the local urban level. As Gough (1979) shows, between 1971 and 1975 the gap between public expenditure and revenue widened to 11% of GNP, requiring state borrowing of £11 billion in 1975, during a period of high inflation, unemployment and falling industrial production. The fiscal crisis was also experienced during the period of the Social Contract, a time when an increase in either direct or indirect taxation was not a possibility. In its attempt to control public expenditure, the unitary state in Britain has had the constitutional capacity to contain the fiscal crisis centrally, by increasing its powers over local government and health-service spending and by more direct intervention in the management of public services.

Changes in the economy at this time provided the conditions for legitimation to be given to the different ideological explanations of the new right and for their different set of solutions to economic problems. As in the United States, the attention of the new right has focused on state clients, state welfare workers and particularly the activities of the militant public-employee unions who were perceived to be one of the main causes of the fiscal crisis (see also Chapter 7).

In both the UK and the US the increased strength and activities of public employees have therefore contributed to and heightened a climate of opinion in which state workers and the state-dependent population are seen as unproductive burdens on wealth creation. However, differences in taxation levels and in collective bargaining for public employees' wage levels have meant that in Britain tax protests at the local level have never been as intense as those in the United States. Tax protests have rather been conducted at a national level, orchestrated by the mass media and politicians, as the welfare state 'was constructed as a populist folk devil' (Hall 1979).

In addition to the increased rate of taxation and economic conflicts of interest then, there are a number of ideological elements in the conflicts of interests between those in the different production sectors, including the scapegoating of 'welfare scroungers' and public sector workers, especially those who are seen to take industrial action against the 'national interest' as in the 'winter of discontent' in 1979 (Dunleavy 1980b).

LABOUR RELATIONS IN THE RECESSION

The United States

In the US, at the end of the 1970s, the corporations in the core industries were faced with declining productivity and increasing international competition especially in certain industries such as the car and steel industries; government deregulation in other industries such as airlines and transport, and increasing non-union competition as a result of the decline of union organization. These conditions have led to a number of significant developments in employer strategies within the strongly unionized industries, starting with the concession bargaining of Chrysler and the United Auto Workers in 1979. Concession bargaining provides for 'give backs' of workers, such as wage freezes and the elimination of cost-of-living adjustments, in return for mainly non-economic concessions and moratoriums on plant closures.

According to Davis, in 1982 concessionary bargaining affected a quarter of unionized plants in the US, and 'during the first half of 1982, almost 60% of the unions bargaining with employers accepted real wage freezes or reductions in their contracts' (Davis 1982). From 1984 onwards unionized private sector workers have received smaller wage and benefit increases than those in the non-unionized sectors of the country *(Monthly Labor Review,* January 1986).

Some commentators have suggested that considerable union gains are included in the trade-offs for these concessions, for example, profit sharing, union membership on boards of directors and guarantees .of income security (Kassalow 1984). Others such as Burawoy (1985), however, refer to these new conditions as a regime of 'new despotism', and Davis (1982) claims that many unions are now refighting battles begun decades earlier. The willingness of union leaders to grant concessions to employers, and accept the management viewpoint, reflects the more general weakening of the bargaining power of workers in the unionized sector, through the increasing decline of union membership and the restructuring of the labour force. The confinement of class conflict to the workplace, rather than the wider political arena, however, means that unionized workers are more dependent on their employers, and enterprise collective bargaining for many welfare benefits. In the face of plant closures and mass lay-offs they are therefore more vulnerable and less protected from the harshness of unemployment.

Alternative forms of work organization and job redesign have also been adopted by many of the large unionized corporations. These have involved 'participatory' work schemes aimed at securing the workers' compliance with management aims. The schemes, often influenced by Japanese management systems, include quality of working life programmes, quality circles, management-labour committees, and profit-sharing. As several writers have argued, these schemes not only contribute to lower unit costs of labour but also improve the flexibility of labour and hence counteract the rigidities of work organization and product markets derived from earlier periods of scientific management techniques (e.g. Coombs 1985, Littler 1985). Intense foreign competition and the trend to computer-based production systems, requiring greater flexibility of labour and products, threaten those industries based on mass production techniques around which the American unions built their power. Whilst unions were able to extract considerable trade-offs from the 'minutely differentiated, contractually codified, internal labour markets' (Davis 1982) of earlier Taylorist regimes, the effect of these new forms of work design would seem to be to reduce the adversarial role of unions as they are integrated within managerial aims.

With the decline of the large industrial unions, the public sector unions have appeared as the only sector with membership growth which could take an innovative role in the labour movement in the US, including a commitment to political action. Davis (1982) notes that in the lower ranks of the trade unions it is the public sector unions which are most politicized and where social democratic currents have gained ground. Women's expanded role in the public sector unions has also meant that the unions have addressed economic and social issues of concern to women, for example pressure for enforcement of affirmative action and equal opportunity employment policies and pressure for the concept of pay equity or 'comparative worth' (Bell 1985). But public employers have often taken a tougher stance with their unions, starting with the 'give backs' of public unions in New York in 1975 which have since been adopted by many state and local governments, as well as the federal government.

Public employing authorities have also used a number of other strategies which include more widespread forms of privatization of publicly owned services than in Britain. Another has concerned the devolution of formerly federally administered welfare services to the state level, which as Raynor (1981) notes could, in the more conservative states or those under financial pressure, destroy the liberal and more egalitarian policy intentions of earlier federal legislation. Reductions in public services have come from the reductions in the federally funded block grants to the state and local governments. In addition the public sector unions were given a salutary and punitive lesson by Reagan when the Professional Air Traffic Controllers' Organization was destroyed by executive order and its entire membership dismissed. Although at the time of writing there are few studies of labour management relations in the public sector in the 1980s, it has been suggested that the fate of PATCO has encouraged public management toughness elsewhere (Mitchell 1983).

The decentralized and fragmented nature of control of public expenditure, management control and collective bargaining in the public sector has affected the ability of the public unions to build up a national strength. Strike activity in the public sector has also continued to be of a shorter duration and to involve less workers than its counterpart in the private sector and, despite the fall of pay relative to the private sector, strike activity has declined in the 1980s. Nor do the public unions have the political resources of public sector unions in Britain (see the last section of this chapter). Although there are links between public sector leaders and the Democratic Party, the Democratic Party itself seems to be advocating policies not dissimilar to those of the Republicans or favouring a strategy of re-industrialization, a business-led corporatism, along the lines of the solution to the fiscal crisis of New York in 1975, which advocated government intervention in support of corporate interests and profits.

Britain

In Britain the main protagonist of change against the trade unions has been the government, which since 1979 has attempted to restructure industrial relations in a number of ways. First, the government has pursued a policy of weakening the strength of the unions; second, this strategy has been implemented in the private sector only indirectly through macro-economic policies; third, the government has attempted to reduce the size and influence of public sector unions, although not acting until two years after taking office; and lastly, no attempt has been made to gain union co-operation at the national level (Soskice 1984). A fifth area is the cumulative impact of legislation governing industrial relations, initially as a buttress to the changes achieved in the structure of industrial relations and more recently to actually shape industrial relations.

Soskice shows how in the early years of the Thatcher administration lack of co-ordination between employers and lack of support by the CBI for the government's policies meant that the government was without direct means of pressure on business employers. Two other strategies were therefore used: in the first case, the government set an example in publicly-owned industries, especially British Leyland where management imposed unilateral control, by-passing the shop-steward system. In the second case the government used macro-economic policy to 'force change in the private sector', through monetary and fiscal policies on interest rates, the exchange rates and unemployment. Since then major changes have occurred in plant closures, direct investment abroad, increased subcontracting of supply and service work, an increase in fixed contract employment and of part-time work especially for women, and changes amongst skilled and semi-skilled workers.

In the private sector there is at present incomplete evidence on the restructuring of industrial relations in Britain, but that which exists (Rose and Jones 1985, Edwards 1985, Kelly 1985) suggests that the emphasis has been on work reorganization schemes rather than radical change in industrial relations. Work reorganization involves increased co-operation with union representatives in order to negotiate the new schemes. Edwards' study of senior managers in manufacturing indus-tries confirms this. He found that there had been no syste-matic attack on union organization, and industrial relations remained important to senior managers, but there had been widespread changes in working practices designed to increase the efficiency of labour utilization. Edwards concludes that the rise in consultative approaches in industrial relations suggests that the management of labour is changing to include the securing of workers' compliance with managerial aims (Edwards 1985).

Other reports of the effects of the recession on workplace industrial relations, including shop-steward organization and joint consultation, warn against a simplified interpretation of the shift of power to employers in the past five years (Marchington and Armstrong 1985, Spencer 1985). Although employers have had to react to external economic pressures, this has not determined the outcome of management-labour relations, for resistance from unions can influence the options that management chooses. Also evident is the diversity of policies adopted by management, although in most cases management wished to protect and maintain the credibility and existence of union organization in the workplace (the exception being the actions taken by Murdoch against the print unions). Thompson, however, interprets these processes as 'empty shell'—'the formal mechanisms concealing the very weak position that many union organizations find themselves in and have to accommodate to' (1986, p.12). Many of the changes, as Thompson points out, 'enshrine management's right to manage', a process which, as we discuss below and in Chapter 8, is also occurring in the public service sector.[9]

At a more general level, however, the recomposition of the labour force has been at the expense of male manual workers, with an associated decline in union membership of the craft and large general unions.[10] The new forms of employment that are appearing, namely, part-time work, especially for married women workers, temporary work, fixed-contract employment and self-employed sub-contractors, are not conducive to union organization. Massey has argued that the spatial effects of this recomposition of the labour force has been to weaken worker organization. The development of the multi-plant corporation has fragmented workers in different locations, the traditional centres of union strength have been weakened, and what remain in the private sector of cities, small firms and services, are notoriously difficult to organize. Elsewhere, firms have relocated their operations in areas where workers have traditionally been unorganized, for example, married women in Cornwall, East Anglia and South Wales. In Britain, Massey argues, the public service sector unions remain as the ones that have the strongest links between workers in different parts of the country, as well as with the community at a local level (1984).

However, it is unlikely that the public service sector will, in the future, generate more jobs, for government policies have been aimed at reducing the size of public employment. In the first two years of office the government took seriously the lessons of the 1970-1974 Heath administration and, concerned that the public and private sectors should not unite, treated the public sector with caution. By the time the public sector was under more direct attack the militancy of unions in the private sector had been subdued through unemployment. A number of policies have since been directed at the public services and their unions:

(i) the use of cash limits as an incomes policy, so that for the last three years wage levels for most groups have remained below both the rate of inflation and private sector wage rise.

(ii) the recommodification of welfare services by promoting the provision of private sector services, and by the contracting out of manual or ancillary services. Neither of these have been as widespread as initially intended, although where they have occurred they have had the effect of fragmenting and dividing the workforce and reducing unionization. Women in particular have borne the brunt of the social costs of these policies both as workers and as the main users of the services (see Chapter 8).

(iii) the introduction of private sector management styles and structures into welfare organizations. In some cases this has resulted in attempts to assert new managerial prerogatives and has reduced the tradition of the public sector as a 'good industrial relations' employer. There has also been a greater emphasis on technical rationality, and techniques used by private industry, for example 'efficiency' drives, performance monitoring, cost-benefit techniques, and 'value for money' exercises; these may reduce public accountability and public debate about the purposes of state welfare provision.

(vi) a shift of decision-making procedures from the more democratic processes to the central, regional and non-elected bodies, as for instance in the abolition of the metropolitan councils; (for a fuller discussion of these policies and their ideological sources of influence see Chapters 7 and 8).

Where the government has to work through local management, however, its policies have been constrained by the range of conflicting and often contradictory pressures operating on local management, and in some cases by opposition tactics from local management itself.[11] Important constraints have been the type of political interests that mobilize around particular services, for example in labour-controlled local authorities, especially the large metropolitan cities, and political pressures at a national level. In addition, as we describe in Chapters 7 and 8, managers and workers are also affected by the contradictory effects of incompatible long-term social welfare policies.

For the public service unions, however, it is likely that the 'frontiers of control' are now being pushed back in a number of areas. Privatization of services through contracting out for instance has been conducted at a local level under the control of local management, and its fragmented and decentralized nature has left national union leaders at a loss as to how to deal with it.[12] The introduction of new management arrangements also means that new managerial prerogatives are being applied which attempt to remove the consensus agreements built up in labour relations in the 1970s, and in this managers are helped by changes in industrial relations legislation. The public sector unions have also lost members in the past six years, through redundancies and reductions in staffing levels, through the contracting out of services and by the more successful recruiting drives of professional bodies.

Nevertheless, in a number of areas the public service unions have a greater national strength and organization, and therefore potential role within the labour movement of the country than is the case in the US. For instance, the centralized control of pay determination in the public sector and the differential application of an incomes policy to the public sector and not the private sector, has affected the extent of industrial conflict in this sector during the 1980s. Throughout the 1980s (with the exception of 1983) the number of working days lost, and the number of workers involved in strike activity in the public service sector was greater than the proportion of employment in that sector, although for private sector industries and services, strike activity has dropped to the lowest level in fifty years. The nature of public service work also leads to forms of action short of striking which do not show up in such statistics.

However, in addition to industrial strategies and because the public unions are 'inextricably emmeshed in political activity', (Batstone *et al.* 1984) the use of political strategies and the extent to which they can mobilize public interests and support have also been an important resource[13]. Since support for state welfare services remains high in Britain amongst all social groups (Taylor-Gooby 1985), the unions have been able to draw on greater sources of support for their opposition, and together with other groups within the labour movement have directed continuous political pressures on government (see Chapter 8 for evidence in the NHS). In line with the suggestion made earlier (p.123) the conditions in which public employment expanded in Britain have conferred a greater legitimacy on state provision of welfare, giving the public service unions much greater political resources than their counterparts in the United States.

CONCLUSION

The sector model developed by O'Connor and the critical theorists has been applied in this chapter as a means of interpreting the growth and militancy of state workers as an aspect of their contradictory location within a sector which is governed by non-market criteria. Using this model it has been possible to distinguish the relationship between workers in the public sector and the private and especially the monopoly sector, as well as the ideological and economic conflicts of interest between workers in each sector.

O'Connor's claim that public sector unions would lead to more direct political involvement and active industrial militancy by public service unions has been borne out in both the UK and the US. In both countries such militancy has implicated the unions in the fiscal crisis of the state, the dominant interpretation of the crisis putting the blame on welfare workers, unions, and clients, and has led to subsequent attempts by governments to weaken the influence of these unions. As the economic conditions of Britain and America changed in the early 1980s, industrial conflict within the private sector unions has been further 'immunized', through the 'give backs' of the American unions or the introduction of new forms of work organization which elicit the compliance and consent of unions in the large corporations. The locus of industrial, and potentially social and political conflict, has shifted to the public sector of each country, where the unions have been the main source of growth and militancy, and when links with client and other social movements are made possible innovation in the labour movement.

As we have discussed however, differences in class action

and mobilization have affected patterns of collective bargaining and state intervention both in the provision of welfare services and in the regulation of labour relations in the two countries. In turn these differences have shaped the extent to which employers have been able to extract concessions from unionized workers and deploy a more flexible workforce. These concessions have been greater in America, since unionized workers are more dependent on their employers for welfare benefits and hence have more to lose when out of work. The welfare services which provided the expansion of public employment in the 1960s in the United States do not protect the unionized population and this suggests that the conflicts of interest between workers in the monopoly sector and public sector in the United States is, therefore, greater, than in Britain, and affect the potential role of public sector unions in the labour movement of the country.

NOTES

1. Considerable attention has recently been given to the political economy of industrial relations, in which the institutional framework which governs industrial relations is seen to be a reflection of the distribution of power and of the mobilization of resources by employers, labour movements and the state. From this perspective comparative analyses have looked at the particular forms in which capitalism developed in different countries, and the characteristics of that development, for example, the timing and speed of its development, recruitment of the labour force, and ownership concentration. Within these structural constraints the particular strategies pursued and choices made by the different groups within each country are considered to lead to the diversity of patterns of industrial relations between the countries (see for example Shalev 1981, Edwards 1983a).
2. Habermas (1976), Offe (1976) and O'Connor (1973) have developed a sectoral model which enables them to comprehend the different relations of production according to the forms of organizational logic governing state and private sectors. These sectors are briefly:

   (i) a private monopoly sector, characterized by highly capital-intensive productions, organized sales markets, national and international operations, strong unionization and high wage rates;

   (ii) a private competitive sector characterized by small firms which are price takers in competitive markets, labour-intensive, with low levels of productivity improvement, low unionization and employment instability;

(iii) A state service sector which is labour-intensive, with low levels of productivity improvement except by employment growth, political determination of wage rates and (in the UK) centralization of wage bargaining;

(iv) Dunleavy (1980a) and Thompson and Beaumont (1978) further divide the state sector to include a public corporation sector which consists mainly of nationalized industries, similar to the private monopoly sector in that they are governed to some extent by market principles, but have greater political determination of wage levels, pricing policies and investment programmes.

(v) Habermas and Offe add a residual labour power sector consisting of the state-dependent population, which is also in part a source of reserve labour and a secondary labour market.

3. The decline in union membership and the weakening of collective bargaining arrangements in the private sector is not unique to the US and the UK, as evidence from the ILO shows that these trends are also occurring in most industrialized market economies (Pankert 1985). The post-war increase in membership of public service unions and the recent increase in the frequency and scale of strikes in the public service is similarly a characteristic of many other countries.

4. The increase in public union militancy in the large north-eastern cities in the United States appears to have been related to the expansion of public expenditure through the federal aid programmes from the mid-1960s. Here the newly and more strongly organized unions used this economic opportunity to push for higher wage claims, better working conditions and fringe benefits (Walsh 1982). Rising prices and the high visibility of private corporate sector wage levels also cintributed to the increased industrial action. Elsewhere public union strikes were often over union recognition or collective bargaining rights, which once obtained led to action for economistic ends.

5. Most strike activity takes place in the NE metropolises, as in the labour movement generally, and also tends to be concentrated amongst particular groups; the teachers, for example, account for 50% of strikes in any one year. Moreover, public employees also participate in strikes less frequently and for shorter periods than those in the private sector of the US (Kearney 1984).

6. Major disputes in the public sector in Britain, therefore, have a significant impact on the overall strike activity for any one year. This is not to say, however, that local disputes and local industrial action in the British public sector have not been important, for often large national disputes have been preceded by local action and more recently considerable action has been taken with regard to local issues such as hospital or school closures.

7. Friedland (1981) argues that policies aimed at the provision of public services and employment are located in agencies which are relatively accessible to voting publics, but policies aimed at sustaining invest-

ment are located in agencies to which popular access is difficult while access by private investors is unhampered.

8. Peretz (1982) has contended that there was no tax revolt, for in California where Proposition 13 was passed there were as many pro-tax reforms passed at the same time as anti-tax reforms, but the former were ignored by the media. The alleged tax revolt, he argues, was a product of the media, and was responsible for the subsequent rise in popular dissatisfaction with paying taxes. Nevertheless, the effect of the alleged tax revolts has been that in those states which have since imposed tax and expenditure limitations, there have been large reductions in public jobs and services.

9. Wage rises in manufacturing industries have, despite a 25% reduction in employment, been growing at an annual rate of 9% and have increased the wage differences between the unionized and non-unionized sections of the workforce. This is interpreted by Thompson as one factor behind the new management strategies as they concede something in return for work restructuring (1986, p.12).

10. In Britain the level of unionization has fallen substantially during the recession from 55% of the workforce in 1979 to around 45% in 1986.

11. Walsh has said of local government staffing levels, for example, that 'central government's influence over local government employment is mainly general, negative and indirect' operating only through general control over finance. (1985, p.115). The ability of central government to influence the local delivery of services in the NHS is also limited, mainly through the dominance of professional providers at local level. Moreover, as we show in Chapter 8, the former management consensus teams in the NHS were initially resistant to contracting out of ancillary services, prompting the government to make contracting out compulsory and to introduce new management arrangements, new terms of contract and salary additions to effect managerial compliance with central policies.

12. The unions are caught in a dilemma, for if the private contractors win, wages and conditions of their members will be lowered and the union's influence removed; if the in-house tender wins, local union leaders will have collaborated in achieving lower conditions of work and possibly lower wages for their members (see Chapter 8).

13. With reference to the political strategies of trade unions Batstone *et al.* have said 'In the private sector success rests primarily on the ability to endanger the employer's profits. In the public sector . . . success rests primarily on the ability of unions to influence the political environment within which they and their employers operate (1984, p.188). However, in contrast to those writers who characterize union actions as either industrial or political, (for example Shalev 1981) Batstone *et al.* point out that public sector unions use both political and industrial strategies (1984, p.303).

7 The Restructuring of Welfare Work I: The New Right and Welfare Policies

This chapter examines the ideological and political practices of governments in the UK and US in the 1980s, as they have attempted to limit the scope and legitimacy of state welfare provision. The restructuring of the welfare state has to be understood in the context of the structural role of the state as well as specific political policies and practices. In Chapter 6 we have seen how in, Britain, the 1974-1979 Labour government responded to the fiscal crisis of the mid-1970s by attempts to restrict the growth of public expenditure, whilst in the US cutbacks in public expenditure and employment took place primarily at the level of the large metropolitan cities. These fiscal crises and government responses to them contributed to the conditions in the late 1970s under which the ideological shifts to the right and the political realignments supporting them took place. In the 1980s, however, a qualitative dimension has been added to the restructuring of the welfare state (Gough 1983) in which specific political and ideological elements of the Conservative and Reagan administrations have sought to roll back the state, transfer activity from the public to the private sector and remove the consensus on which the post-war collective provision was based. At the same time as stressing the virtues of a return to market economy principles, values which reassert individual and family responsibility are also exhorted. The set of ideas which have influenced the policies of the Reagan and Thatcher governments are discussed in the first section of this chapter. The second section examines specific welfare policies and governments' attempts to implement them.

The formulation of state policies however takes place in the absence of market criteria, and in a context of a diffusion of objectives in public policy making, political pressures and interest-group demands, as well as budgetary constraints. As was argued in Chapter 3, the state, therefore, has 'a deficient planning capacity, characterized by a vacillation of policies, a muddling through and a reactive avoidance of crises' (pp.55). Moreover, the different economic and political demands may be non-commensurate and have contradictory effects for governments, state managers and workers. In this context state managers face particular difficulties in devising appropriate structures of control which make compatible these conflicting pressures. The third part of this chapter examines the context of state welfare and the effects of these non-commensurate policies on the changing organization of welfare in the US and the UK. Examples are taken from health care in the US and from the NHS and social services in Britain.

The outcome of government policies directed to restructuring the welfare state are however uncertain, for these strategies are likely to meet with resistance and opposition from those groups whose interests are threatened. As we argued in Chapter 2 the changes in the organization of work are not solely achieved through the imposition of management control structures, but are the outcome of the continual interaction between management's and employees' intentions and resistances at the level of the workplace and in the wider economic and political spheres.

This theme is picked up in the next chapter with reference to the implementation of recent government policies in the NHS in Britain. The introduction of new management structures based on private sector principles, and the imposition of a privatization programme in the NHS, are examined through two case studies. As we shall see the imposition of these new control structures generates further contradictions which must in turn be resolved.

THE NEW RIGHT

Themes Within the New Right

The set of ideas which have been labelled the new right consists of a number of different and sometimes conflicting theoretical strands of thought. It is not the intention here to examine the theoretical validity of these ideas, or their development and ascendancy or to discuss the differences between neo-liberal economic ideas and forms of neo-conservatism, for these have been admirably written about elsewhere (see for example, Bosenquet 1983, Peele 1984, and Levitas 1986). Rather the following discussion briefly outlines the different themes within the new right and their sources of influence on the Reagan and Thatcher administrations.

In all strands of thought in the new right, there is a general agreement that promotion of the market is the most appropriate mechanism for the new economic management. State activities and expenditure are seen to impose a burden of taxation and regulation which are 'disincentives to investment' of capital on the one hand, whilst state benefits, citizen rights and the gains of the collective power of labour are a 'disincentive to work' for labour on the other. One strand of theory, known as the 'economics of politics' or public choice theory, uses a model of the market economy to explain and analyse the growth of state expenditure and activities (for example, Downs 1957, Buchanan and Wagner 1977, and Tullock 1976). Political 'markets' are seen as similar to behaviour in the economic market, that is, political parties compete with each other for votes in the same way as businesses compete for customers. In the post-war period this has led to ever-increasing expectations from the electorate, and increasing promises from politicians who bid up voters' expectations.

In addition, demands from competing interest groups also succeed in expanding government expenditures. State bureaucrats too are a further pressure on state growth, since they have a sectional interest in maximizing the size of their budgets. State employees also increase public expenditure since the expansion of welfare programmes enhances their opportunities for higher incomes and career advancement.

Once created, this 'ratchet effect' tends to perpetuate state welfare programmes and agencies, but instead of promoting the public interest these activities, it is claimed, protect and support the private interests of state workers, professionals and officials. The result is an over supply of government services, 'Expenditure soars, bureaus expand and governments become more and more inclined to intervene in the market economy' (Gamble, in Levitas 1986, p.44).

Allied to these views is the notion of 'overloaded government', a neo-liberal interpretation of the fiscal crisis of the state. Overloaded government theories stem from earlier pluralist perspectives, and see the demands on government from the competing interest groups and electoral expansion as far exceeding the capacity of the government to meet them, especially in conditions of economic recession, as occurred in the mid-1970s (for example Crozier 1975). Economic growth in the 1950s and 1960s allowed inflation to serve as a distributional vent for the excessive demands which were channelled through the state. In the economic conditions of the 1970s 'in the face of claims from business groups, labour unions, and the beneficiaries of government largesse, it becomes difficult if not impossible for democratic governments to curtail spending, income and increase taxes and control prices and wages' (Crozier 1975). Weak governments unable to deny these demands push up the levels of public expenditure beyond revenues collected from taxation.

Increased public expenditure and public employment, it was further argued by Bacon and Eltis (1976), overburden or 'crowd out' the private and productive sector. Britain has too few producers in goods and services which are marketed, but this sector increasingly has to finance the expanded non-marketed public sector. There was obviously a need, it was argued, not only to cut the size of the public sector, but to roll back the expectations of the electorate and pressure groups, except when performance of the public sector could be stepped up. This would, however, involve 'firm' and 'decisive' political leadership that is less responsive to democratic pressures (Held 1984).

Other strands of neo-liberal thought see the market mechanism as the most important principle to be supported;

Friedman and Hayek represent different theoretical strands of this tradition. In neo-liberal economics, which has its origins in nineteenth-century laissez-faire ideas, economic freedom is seen as the condition of political freedom. The role of the state is reduced to that of the nightwatchman and individuals can exercise choice in the allocation of their income; they are less dependent on the state and can exercise self-help, individual responsibility and initiative. Monetarism can be seen as a narrowly technical economic policy which fits logically together with neo-laissez-faire doctrines, since monetarist diagnosis and prescriptions work more smoothly when the 'invisible hand' of the market is operating. Friedman's monetarism, for example, has played an influential role in the Thatcher government and links the quantity of money in the economy with prices and hence with the determination of inflation. This implies that the money supply must be controlled, which can be done through limiting government expenditure; the imposition of cash limits and control of the PSBR for instance are attempts to do this.

In the US, supply-side economics has been more influential in the Reagan administration, which has concentrated on the supply of labour input to the economy, and the necessity to lower taxes and wage rates to provide incentives. Supply-side economics also asserts that government expenditures and a high tax burden are a weight on economic growth; the government role then becomes that of unleashing the supply of goods and services in the economy by stimulating private sector activity through the incentives created.

Source of Influence on the Thatcher and Reagan Administrations

In Britain, the new right's influence on the Conservative party was channelled through a number of research institutes, pressure groups and individuals within the party, for example the Institute of Economic Affairs (1957), the Centre for Policy Studies set up by Sir Keith Joseph in 1974, Aims of Industry (1942) The Adam Smith Institute (1979) and the National Association for Freedom (1975). As Levitas points out these groups have merely taken over from others which date back to the nineteenth century: 'private capital has always defended itself against socialism and the labour movement in this way'. For individual politicians, the defeats of the Conservative government under Heath in 1974 'deeply scarred the memories of some of their members . . . leaving a policy and personality vacuum into which advocates of Friedmanite policies stepped' (Heald 1983, p.9). The achievement of Thatcher though, has been to popularize the views of the new right, converting them into a 'housekeeping' common sense, which had appealed to the electorate and to Conservative politicians. The outcome has 'allowed the new right project to become installed as a framework within which thinking about policy could go ahead' (Gamble, in Levitas 1986, p.49).

In the US, Peele found that the new right's influence on politics stemmed from a series of alliances on the right in the late 1970s, and the coming together of a range of pressure groups, think tanks, and individual politicians. She comments:

The neo-conservatives, free marketeers, and supply siders—and indeed other critics of the existing pattern of government policies such as the increasingly influential public choice theorists—obviously operated to a large extent in the somewhat rarefied atmosphere of the universities, research centres and think tanks. Developments in conservative circles at a more routine level of political organization produced in addition a movement which will here be labelled the new right. The range of single issue groups, institutions and individuals to whom this label was applied proved increasingly successful during the 1970s in getting their chosen issues onto the political agenda and in creating the impression that the issues which mattered to the American people were conservative ones' (Peele 1985, p.7).

These new right influences have committed the Reagan and Thatcher administrations to (i) reducing the size and expenditure of the state sector, (ii) reducing the levels of taxation, (iii) leaving labour markets to regulate themselves, (iv) weakening what are perceived as over-powerful unions and professions so that their restrictive practices and monopoly control are removed and the supply and price of labour is subjected to competitive forces, (v) promoting the operation of market mechanisms through various forms of privatization, (vi) increasing individual and family self-help, responsibility and initiative, so that people are not dependent on the state or its professional providers, and expectations and aspirations of state welfare services are rolled back. Given the contradictory whole of the state, however, the success of governments in achieving these aims is limited by the fact that, as we noted in Chapter 3, these policies are still costly for state budgets and 'still take place under social arrangements which are themselves external to the [market]' (Offe 1975b). As several commentators have argued, the costs of forcing the market to be free are: a strong state, increased centralized intervention and more authoritarian and repressive measures (Held 1984, Gamble 1986). These points are developed below in the discussions in the next section on the implementation of social policies, and in the last part of the chapter on the contradictory effects of the changing organization of welfare.

WELFARE POLICIES IN THE 1980s

The Reagan and Conservative administrations have made attempts to reduce public expenditure through tighter financial controls over public agencies. In the US, economic policies have concentrated on supply-side economics and the lowering of tax rates rather than reducing the large federal budget deficit. Lower taxes have favoured the corporations, and personal tax cuts of 23% over three years have favoured the wealthy—this has been estimated to be equivalent to a loss of $750 billion to the Treasury over five years and has necessitated major cuts in domestic public expenditure (Peele 1986, p.154). Carroll *et al.* have also noted that the large federal budget deficit has been used instrumentally as an imperative of expenditure control. 'Reduction of the deficit over an extended period gives the president the tools he needs for central control over public policy' (Carroll *et al.* 1985).

Overall, however, the objective of reducing state expenditure has not been achieved; total general government expenditure grew from 32.7% of GNP in 1979 to 37.5% in 1986. Within the federal budget, however, there has been a transfer of funds from social welfare programmes to military spending, the funding of state agencies of law and order, and state aid to private enterprise. Defence spending, for example, grew by just over 1% of GNP between 1981 and

1985, whilst non-defence programmes have been cut by 0.6%, and the federal debt interest cost has risen by 1.25% of GNP (OECD Economic Survey USA 1985/6 p.26). A key element of Reagan's domestic strategy has also been to reduce the states' and local governments' dependence on federal funding and federal responsibility for welfare programmes. As levels of federal aid to state and local governments have declined, the Great Society programmes set up in the 1960s by the federal government have been cut or removed. As many states are unresponsive to the needs of poor families and minority groups, it is these groups that have borne the costs of the policy.

In the UK tighter financial controls have been achieved by the use of cash limits as a control on the total budget of each service and, additionally, the use of cash limits as an incomes policy with respect to public sector wage levels. In local government, centralized financial controls have taken the form of the 'block grant' system and in 1983 the rate-capping scheme, which prevents local authorities from raising taxes beyond the level determined by central government. As in the US, though, public expenditure has continued to grow despite the government's efforts to curb it. There has also been a transfer of funds within the total budget, as defence and law and order budgets have increased more than social expenditure, but social expenditure has also continued to rise. For example, O'Higgins and Patterson show that the defence and law and order budgets which took about 14.5% of public expenditure in 1978-1979 accounted for 17% in 1983-1984. The social security budget, however, which includes payments for unemployment and employment services, grew from 25% in 1978-1979 to almost 30% in 1983-1984. Diverse political and other pressures have meant that expenditure related to social programmes has also continued to rise, for example, health and social services have increased slightly, although education has slightly declined: 'The share of social expenditure [defined as education, health, social services, social security, housing and employment services] therefore increased from about 55% of public expenditure in 1978/9 to 57% in 1983/4' (O'Higgins and Patterson 1985). Although the government has had a lack of success in controlling social expenditure there has, nevertheless, been financial stringency for most welfare services and, in different service areas, underfunding or actual reductions in service. Levels of public expenditure have not been sufficient to meet the needs of the changing population structure, and increased social needs and deprivations.

A second strategy in the restructuring of welfare work has involved changes in the internal management and control of welfare organizations. Management policies in the federal administration in the US have been termed supply-side management as a 'logical corollary to supply side economics' (Carroll *et al.* 1985). The major components of this management approach show similarities with those adopted by the Conservative administration in Britain, and are to be found in decisions on budgeting and financial management, in the reduction in the collection and dissemination of information, (as Carroll *et al.* point out, information can be used to show 'need' and to provide rationalizations for new programmes), in reduction of staff, in the promotion of business practices in public agencies, and in private sector initiatives. In both countries too there is the paradox of policies of decentralization of state programmes to lower tiers of the state, but increasing centralization of controls (for example see p.155 for the US and p.163 for the UK).

Attempts to impose tighter management controls on welfare work include the introduction of private sector styles of management, and an increased emphasis on technical rationality to increase efficiency and the productivity of labour in welfare organizations. In the UK, examples of purposive rational techniques include 'value for money' exercises under the Audit Commission, 'efficiency saving' schemes under Raynor scrutinies, increased performance monitoring, and cost-improvement schemes (see Chapter 8 section one).[1] Schemes which import business methods into the public sector are not new, and earlier failures of managerialism are indicative of the difficulties central government has faced in influencing local management and the actual delivery of services.

Such techniques tend to concentrate only on inputs to the services, and the quality or effectiveness of welfare services—

which are difficult to cost or measure since they are not marketable—are ignored. Discussions about the provision of local welfare or health needs of the community increasingly become technical judgements about the increased efficiency of commercial transactions. As Heald notes, such techniques conflict with principles of equity embodied in public services, and may distort and undermine the initial and often multiple welfare aims of the service (1983).

The application of technical rationality is however instrumental for the state, for since these techniques do not take account of the quality or effectiveness of welfare provision, evidence relating to the effects of government policies on welfare services is obscured from public knowledge or debate.[2] To the extent that increased technical rationality reduces public discussion about the purposes and outcomes of welfare, the scope for the state to impose its policies and more coercive controls is enhanced.

A third strategy which has been promoted by the Reagan and Thatcher administrations is that of the privatization of services that is 'responsibility for a particular service transfers to the private sector, or market criteria, such as profit or the ability to pay are used to ration or distribute benefits and services' (Walker 1984, p.25). Privatization can take many forms; Heald (1983) for example notes four:

Privatization of the financing of a service which continues to be produced by the public sector, for example, levying charges on users.

Privatization of the production of a service which continues to be financed by the public sector, for example, contracting out of services, or the use of vouchers for purchase of service.

Denationalization and load-shedding, that is the selling off of public enterprises, and the transfer of state functions to the private sector, for example in the US the employment of social workers by private companies, or the private practice of social workers (Weddell 1986).

Liberalization, the removal of statutory barriers which prevent the private sector from competing for markets against the public sector, for example, in the UK the abolition of the Fair Wages Resolution in the tendering of services for contract (see also Chapter 8); in the US deregulation of the federal government's monitoring role has been central to the philosophy of the Reagan administration (see Peele 1984, pp.161-3).

Privatization is, however, a particularly attractive policy for the Reagan and Conservative administrations for it is considered to subject state agencies to the disciplines of the market, provide profitable markets for private companies, and weaken the strength of the public sector unions.[3] As was argued in Chapter 3, however, privatization is one way in which the state, in the context of conflicting and contradictory pressures, may seek to reduce the difficulties it faces in devising appropriate structures of control in public welfare organizations. But the implementation of privatization programmes exacerbates (as we shall see in Chapter 8) these difficulties by generating further problems, oppositions and contradictions for state managers. The expansion of different schemes of private welfare also increases the financial costs of the state (Taylor-Gooby 1985 pp.79-87) and long-term social costs are generated through increased social inequalities (Le Grand and Robinson 1984).

THE CONTRADICTIONS OF THE CHANGING ORGANIZATION OF WELFARE

The conflicting and diffuse economic and political pressures operating on the state make the formulation of strategies in welfare organizations more difficult and complex than in the private sector.[4] In addition to the control strategies of governments, such as those outlined above, social welfare policies also have to be implemented which are orientated to social needs or to social welfare criteria and are not designed with reference to the control of labour. Nevertheless, as we discuss below, such policies can have consequences for the conditions and content of work and the employment of workers. In addition, many of the effects of government policies do not stem solely from recent short-term policies, but also from 'long term policies either deriving from plans for expansion or from problems that arose in this expansion' (Manson 1979). The discussion below examines the effects of these incom-

patible policies and political pressures on the changing organization of welfare work, first with respect to health care in the
US, and second, for the NHS and social services in the UK.

Health Care in the US

In the US, state action to provide a minimum level of health
insurance for the poor and elderly sections of the population
has, paradoxically, promoted the growth of medicine as the
country's second largest profit-making industry in the 1980s.
State funded health insurance was extended to, and has benefited, the elderly and poor sections of the population in the
1960s as a result of the struggles of social movements during
that period. With the introduction of Medicare and Medicaid,
many of the newly insured began to use the more prestigious
voluntary non-profit hospitals, instead of the poorer public
hospitals they had previously used. Since then public
spending on these programmes has soared, so that the federal
government is now the largest single financier of medical care,
although that care is mainly delivered through the private
sector. The US now has the highest per capita per GDP
spending on health in the OECD countries, but many poor
Americans remain uninsured: in the late 1970s, 26.6 million or
one eighth of the population were uninsured, whilst by the
middle 1980s 38% of the population were uninsured. The US
also compares unfavourably with other countries on health
status indicators, showing the poorest health status of the
advanced countries (Heidenheimer *et al.* 1983, Navarro 1985,
OECD 1985/6).

The growing numbers of elderly people, increasing
numbers of those eligible for Medicaid and the use and development of high-technology medicine have contributed to
the increased costs of health care. But for the main reason for
the increase in costs has been the method of delivering health
care through third-party insurance, for the more a hospital
spent on patients the more they were re-imbursed: 'To attract
patients the voluntary hospitals sought the best known specialists and allowed them freedom in the purchase of medical
equipment' (Raynor 1983, pp.51). Although the non-profit
hospitals did not themselves make profits, their expansion in
the 1960s and 1970s benefited the private sector, contributing

to the profits of drug, equipment, supplies and construction companies servicing the hospitals.

Non-profit hospitals now face considerable competition from for-profit hospitals, whose numbers have grown to more than a thousand in twenty years. Thirty-five major companies are now providing private health care, although there is a monopoly of control by four companies.[4] As Raynor observes, what is new here is not the 'introduction of profit seeking behaviour into American medicine—that had always been there—but the intervention of the new medical corporations and their business methods' (1984, p.19). Management of profit hospitals has greater administrative control over physicians, so that decisions can be made on the basis of corporate interests rather than in the interests of the physicians or health care (McKinley and Arches 1985). For-profit hospitals are therefore less encumbered in introducing business management control structures, production and marketing techniques in order to reduce their costs. Non-profit hospitals have responded to the competition by adopting the corporations' management techniques, or by contracting out the management of the hospital to the corporations.[5]

Public hospitals have become an underfunded and under-developed sector, used by poor or uninsured people. Their decline has been affected by the expansion of the non-profit hospitals, by closures and redundancies in the large cities during the fiscal crisis of the mid-1970s, and now by the expansion of private hospitals. In the belief that private management reduces hospital costs, local officials are also increasingly employing private contractors in the management of public hospital services.[6]

Paradoxically, however, although health provision is a large and expanding market for private firms, the corporations have called for measures to limit the costs of health care. The reason for this is that employers in the monopoly sector pay high employee health benefits in wages, which have become a major cost in production, and the health costs of retired workers in particular are an increasing financial liability to the corporations. The accelerating rise in health expenditures by the state, (health care now costs the federal government 10.5% of GNP), has also led to pressure from business groups and the new right for costs to be reduced. Health-care cost containment has therefore become one of the principal priorities of the Reagan administration.

Payments for Medicaid and Medicare have been the principal targets for cuts, as eligibility has been reduced and the amounts individuals have to pay have been increased. Contrary to the Reagan administration's commitment to free market principles and reductions in government regulation, a centralist system of price controls for Medicare patients has been introduced. This scheme establishes a prospective payment system (PPS), in which the amount paid for treatment is predetermined by the patient's diagnostic group (DRG), regardless of what the treatment actually costs. The principle behind pre-paid systems is that if the hospital can treat the patient for less cost than the DRG rate, it has made a profit. The new incentive is therefore to save costs to avoid loss. It is in the hospital's interest to treat the patient quickly and for as little resource as possible. There is evidence that hospitals are now using computer models to establish the most profitable DRG cases for their hospital and the specializations they will develop (*Health Service Journal* 3, November 1983). These specializations need have little regard for the health needs of the community and could lead 'to whole communities being without certain basic health services if these prove to be unprofitable in hospitals serving the area' (Dredge 1983). Unprofitable patients, for example, Medicare and Medicaid patients, could be shifted to other hospitals as certain cases are 'cream skimmed'. If they are to survive, then, hospitals have to concentrate on treatment areas which are the most cost-effective and profitable.

Prepaid systems are not new, however, and were an element in the Health Maintenance Organizations (HMOs) introduced in 1973. HMOs have been slow to develop and by 1980 covered about 5% of the population, but as they have been seen by the Reagan administration as a means of promoting competition and containing costs it is anticipated that they will become more widespread. In HMOs doctors have an incentive to keep their patients in hospitals for shorter periods and, if they have a share in any profits realised, they also have an incentive to keep costs as low as possible. If doctors are salaried employees of HMOs, management can exercise greater controls over physicians and other health workers. As Derber shows, there is a potential for all the types of control— ideological, bureaucratic, productivity, and technical—that characterize industrial management to be implemented in HMOs (Derber 1984; see also Chapter 5).

Policy Trends in the NHS and Social Services in Britain

In Britain many of the effects of government policies on health and welfare work stem not only from recent policies but also from long-term policies deriving from periods of economic expansion. Of particular importance are strategies of rational planning which now operate in a period of overall limits and reductions in public expenditure. In the 1970s, radical critiques of health care such as the 'inverse care law' or the diminishing returns of high technology (which were pro- moted by the application of technical rationality in the 1960s) were incorporated into government planning policies in the NHS. Such policies sought to redistribute resources more equitably between geographical areas according to geogra- phical variations in health needs (Report of the Resource Allocation Working Party 1976 (DHSS 1976a), or RAWP as it is known), to develop provision for comparatively neglected groups such as the mentally ill, handicapped and elderly, or to develop neglected areas of health care such as primary care and community health (DHSS 1976b).

In a period of financial restraint and underfunding of the health service, the implementation of the RAWP formula has resulted in cutbacks and closures of hospitals in some of the richer regions which also have pockets of social deprivation. London, for instance, because of its prestigious teaching hospitals and a declining population, has been designated as one of the over-provided areas in terms of resources. Under the RAWP criteria London's health authorities have seen their budgets progressively reduced and reallocated to other areas of increasing population and relatively fewer resources. This has resulted in drastic cuts and closures of hospitals, wards and beds, even in the most deprived inner-city boroughs in London. Conflicts over resource distribution now take place between and within different health authorities and hospitals at sub-regional levels rather than between people in the inner-city areas and central government. Other government priority groups—the elderly, handicapped and mentally ill—have also been adversely affected by the financial and employment cuts of 1983/1986 which have meant that health authorities have economized by postponing improvements in care for these groups.

In the social services, the Conservatives, when they took office in 1979, claimed they were adopting a policy of 'disengagement' of the centre from the management of local services. At the same time the Conservatives sought an expanded role for private, non-statutory and voluntary provision of welfare. Social policies for child care, elderly and mentally handicapped people showed, however, a continuity with previous governments especially the 'long standing but ill developed' policy of 'care in the community'. In practice, though, there have been enhanced centralized controls over resources which have made it difficult to achieve these earlier and unrenounced social policies (Webb and Wistow 1982, 1985).

As Webb and Wistow note, these policies are producing a number of contradictory trends. As a result of more stringent financial controls community care has been interpreted by the government as a policy which must find 'low cost solutions', through informal networks of family, friends and neighbours. That the burden of caring falls on women is consistent with the Conservatives' aim of redefining the position of women within the family. But although there has been a shortage of public funds devoted to community care, private residential care has expanded to the extent that there has been 'an unlimited blank cheque drawn on public funds for private sector residential care development' (Henwood 1986). This expansion of private provision has not only been expensive for the state but has concentrated on residential provision which is a substitute for the family and for 'the most needy—those without family support' (Webb and Wistow 1985).

The impact of these policy developments, as many feminist writers have argued, has been disproportionately on women. The expansion of private residential care extends the forms of lower-paid and often part-time work available for women. In local government women form the majority of employees and are therefore vulnerable to redundancies and other cuts which affect their work processes. Women are also the main users of social services provided by local authorities, and cuts in service provision also affect them directly (Webster 1985). The policy of community care for dependent people has also been seen as a policy which directly increases sexual divisions by depending on 'the substantial and consistent input of women's unpaid labour in the home, whilst at the same time effectively excluding them from the labour market and increasing their economic and personal dependence on men' (Finch 1984, p.6).

CONCLUSION

The theme of this chapter has been to examine the ways in which specific political and ideological practices have been directed at state welfare provision, their contradictory effects and their implications for the organization and control of welfare work. Thus the set of ideas which have influenced and sustained the policies of the Reagan and Thatcher administrations were discussed, as well as specific policies directed to the restructuring of the welfare state. The concern of this book with the control of welfare work has meant however that a number of important policy areas of the new conservatism have not been discussed, for example the lack of policies to mitigate the high levels and effects of unemployment, attempts to restructure the labour force (but see Chapters 4 and 7), the new emphasis on the family and women's place within it, issues of racism and the erosion of civil liberties (see Levitas 1986 for a discussion of some of these issues). Within the workings of the international and national economies, these government policies are attempts to transform class, gender and ethnic relations within the US and UK societies. The restructuring of welfare provision is therefore only one theme within this transformation process and will also be affected by the extent of change achieved by the new policy directions.

The success of the Reagan and Thatcher administrations in

achieving their chosen projects is limited however by the different institutional arrangements and constellations of political pressures and struggles within each society. In this respect Peele has remarked

In attempting to put into effect Reagan's brand of radical conservatism, the American President faced difficulties which did not beset contemporary political leaders with similar objectives, such as Margaret Thatcher. For whereas the British system of government has a centralized Cabinet structure and a unified Civil Service and is as a result usually an efficient agent of intervention on domestic politics and a flexible instrument in foreign crisis, the American policy is fragmented and decentralized making it easier to prevent action than to undertake it' (1984, p.147).

Reagan has not pursued in such a single-minded fashion as Thatcher the new conservatism, and after the first year of office has had the opposition of Congress to contend with. However, as we argued in Chapter 7, the legitimation of state welfare programmes is less secure in the US than in Britain, its weak labour movement has been further eroded and, as Davis notes, Reaganism has inherited 'one of the most advantageous balances of power within contemporary world capitalism' (1984a). Reaganism has then had more success in eliciting a popular support for new right policies on social issues 'and has created a synthesis of conservative economics, populism and nationalism which has no exact counterpart in the politics of the right in Europe' (Peele 1984, p.194).

NOTES

1. Raynor scrutinies or 'efficiency savings' were orientated to achieving value for money initially in the Civil Service but later extended to the health service and other public bodies. The stated aim is to achieve the same outputs for fewer inputs, but little attention is given to outputs; rather the studies are interested only in costs. In the Civil Service they have had the effect of reducing staff numbers, introducing costs in some services, transferring costs from the state to employers and, in the health service, the selling of land and staff accommodation.
2. See pp.19-20 of the Committee of Public Accounts 1985/6 'Control of Nursing Manpower' and Hansard for questions asked in the House of Commons to the minister responsible for Health and Social Services.

3. It is assumed by the advocates of the free market that private com-
    panies will be more efficient in meeting activities at present supplied
    by the state, for the companies are single-purpose organizations,
    services can be provided at lower costs and can be more flexible and
    innovative in responding to the needs of recipients. Public welfare
    bureaucracies are portrayed as static and inflexible to changes over
    time and strangled by bureaucratic inertia. The absence of market
    discipline, it is claimed, means that inefficient practices cannot be
    driven out of business or forced to adapt, and the monopoly controls
    of the professions and trade unions mean that hours of work, working
    practices and pay and conditions of work are over-generous and push
    up costs relative to the private sector (see for example Savas 1982).
    However, the study by Schlesinger *et al.* 1986 on competitive bidding
    in mental health services shows that none of these claims can be
    substantiated. They found that (i) the contracting process increases
    administration and bureaucratic rules to monitor and regulate the
    process, (ii) competitive arrangements degenerate into effective
    monopolies for private vendors, (iii) although costs initially fell by the
    lowering of wages and conditions for staff this was only short-term,
    and (iv) competition conflicted with and adversely affected continuity
    and quality of care (see also Radical Statistics Health Group, 1987).
4. Four private corporations now own 75% of private beds. One
    company the Hospital Corporation of America owns three times the
    number of beds as the next largest company, and has expanded so
    rapidly that it is now amongst Fortune magazine's top 500 companies.
    The combined profits of the top four companies increased by 344%
    between 1979 and 1983. (NUPE SCAT 1985).
5. 371 private hospitals now contract out their management services; 325
    of these are non-profit hospitals *(Medicine in Society,* Vol. 12 No. 1,
    1986).
6. Around 180 public hospitals have been bought, leased or managed by
    the private companies *(Medicine in Society,* Vol. 12, No. 1, 1986).

8 The Restructuring of Welfare Work II: The Case of the NHS

This chapter examines recent attempts by the state to restructure welfare organizations, by a discussion of the introduction of market rationality and criteria into the NHS in Britain. The chapter consists of two case studies of the implementation of government policies in the NHS since 1983. In section one the initial effects of the introduction of new NHS management arrangements based on private sector principles are discussed. Section two examines the political imposition of a programme of privatization of ancillary services in the NHS. The case studies draw on research conducted by the author in two district health authorities in a county in south-east England,[1] as well as other empirical studies and secondary sources of data.

The two case studies develop a number of themes discussed earlier in this book. First, with respect to the analysis of the labour process, it was argued in Chapter 2 that the concepts of management strategy and of management control are problematic. In particular the existence of managerial intentions should not be taken as evidence of their successful implementation, for there always exists an indeterminacy of control. Control means are emergent processes produced by the continual interplay between management and worker intentions and resistances (Storey 1985). From this perspective, management is not a homogeneous, rational group whose control strategies flow unimpeded from the top of the hierarchy down to those at subordinate levels, but management has to contend with competing rationales and active resistance within the organization. Management strategy will be the outcome of internal bargaining and conflicts between different sectional groups. The outcomes of these conflicts then require to be translated into specific devices and operational practices to achieve them, and these can in turn produce tensions and practical difficulties which generate instabilities and further conflicts calling for 'coping' strategies on the part of management (Reed 1986). These practical difficulties or failures to implement strategies arise because once managerial decisions are made known they then become the basis on which groups lower down the hierarchy organize their responses and resistance (Wardell 1986). Management not only has to cope with the tensions that such resistance throws up, but must also work at the continual reassertion of control mechanisms over other groups.

Second, the case studies illustrate the nature of the 'political contingencies' operating on both managers and worker groups within a public sector organization (Batstone *et al.* 1984). In attempting to devise and impose new structures of control state managers find themselves faced with a number of diverse, ambiguous and conflicting pressures that stem from the contradictory role of the state in the provision of welfare services (see Chapter 3). In particular there is a contradiction between the requirement to introduce market rationality into public sector organizations in order to relieve the financial problems of governments, increase productivity and remove the politicized nature of state welfare provision, and the requirement to maintain the legitimatory aspects of state welfare services orientated to the welfare needs of the population and as a means of securing mass loyalty to the state's authority. The limits to the state's policy-making role is determined by the undermining of the basis of legitimation (Chapter 3), and as we shall see the public sector unions seek to manipulate these limits as they engage in political forms of action in opposition to the state's and management's policies (Chapter 7). Through the application of technical rationality, however, (in which political issues or practical problems are transformed into technical problems and solutions), state management increases its scope to impose control structures on its internal organizations.

THE INTRODUCTION OF GENERAL MANAGEMENT IN THE NHS

The 1974 reorganization of the NHS created management consensus teams consisting of a doctor, nurse, administrator and treasurer. The consensus teams meant that agreements had to be reached between groups with very different rationales but, as several studies have shown, the primary decision makers remained the medical practitioners (Hunter 1979, Haywood and Alaszewski 1980). In comparison to private sector managers, health managers were relatively powerless and subordinate to professional interests. The dilemma for the government was how to impose its political priorities on an organization where professional judgement determined the local delivery of services.

In its first term of office the government stressed decentralization in the 1982 reorganization of the health service and a rejection of 'overcomplicated and bureaucratic' planning arrangements. One tier of the administrative structure of the NHS was removed and a system of performance monitoring, through regional and district reviews, introduced. Nonetheless, contrary to statements about devolution of the management of the health service, there was evidence of increased centralized controls; namely, the requirement that health regions keep within their cash limits, the withholding of 0.5% of revenue in the form of 'efficiency savings' designed to force health authorities to deliver the same volume of services at lower cost, reductions in manpower targets and budgets in 1983, and the political compulsion to contract out ancillary services. These cuts quickened the pace of closure of wards and hospitals and of rationalizations of labour (although there were wide discrepancies between authorities), and the impact of the cuts was further exacerbated by the application of RAWP criteria (see Chapter 8).

The Griffiths Report
Increased political intervention in the management of the health service was accompanied by the introduction in 1984 of new management arrangements for the NHS. The government appointed, in 1983, a team of businessmen, led by

Griffiths the managing director of the supermarket chain Sainsburys, to give advice on the 'effective use and management of manpower' in the NHS. Their report chose to make recommendations within existing legislation, focusing on the creation of a new management culture and ethos, namely the introduction of a commercial-style management into the health service. The recommendations of the Griffiths Report were that:

(i) The consensus management team should be replaced with a 'general' line manager (from any discipline) at every tier in the health service, who would take responsibility for all decisions at that level. Accountability was to be achieved by extending the review process (established in the 1982 reorganization) through regional and district health authorities. The authorities were also to be given greater freedom to organize their own management structures in the way best suited to local requirements.

(ii) The new general managers should initiate major cost improvement programmes.

(iii) At the centre and part of the DHSS a new NHS Management Board and Health Service Supervisory Board were to be appointed by the Secretary of State.

(iv) Clinicians should be more closely involved in the management process through the introduction of management budgeting.

The Griffiths Report stressed that although the NHS was not concerned with the profit motive there were clear similarities between NHS management and business management, in particular the control of expenditure, levels of service, quality of product, meeting budgets, cost improvement, productivity, and motivating staff. The main problem was that there was no clearly identifiable officer in charge at regional, district or hospital level for 'planning, implementation and control of performance' (p.11).

Despite the fact that the effects of the 1982 reorganization were still in progress, the recommendations of the Griffiths Report were hastily pushed through by the government with little opportunity for consultation with all groups, for example, there were less than thirty-two weeks between the publication of the report and the requirement that health authorities appoint general managers (Carrier and Kendall 1986). The Griffiths report has since been criticized as based on limited and unsystematic evidence and research, for brevity of public debate and consultation, for ignoring the role of public accountability in the NHS and for the assumption that business methods of management are appropriate for a public health service (Carrier and Kendall 1986).

The government wished to appoint the new managers from the private sector, and health authorities were allowed to pay salaries above the Whitley rates. Of the 744 new managers at regional, district and unit levels, only 11%, however, were appointed from outside the NHS and only 5% from the private sector (Hansard 26th June 1986).[2] The Griffiths proposals are, however, central to the government's attempts to implement tighter management and financial controls, and general managers are seen as the key to ensuring the effectiveness of political priorities. The appointments were to be of a fixed-term contract for three years as a way of motivating managers to implement the centrally initiated policies. More recently the DHSS has announced that general managers are to be paid 'discretionary additions' to salary for 'the extent to which they achieve change'; this will include the extent to which hospitals, wards or beds are closed (DHSS 1986). Whilst the terms of contract of the general managers are a means of ensuring that government policies are complied with, the managers themselves are 'caught in a professional stranglehold' (Shuster 1986), for the new management arrangements are based on negative incentives; if the new managers are successful in running an underfunded service and making further cuts, the government will continue to reduce the health service budget.

At the time of writing, many of the general managers had been in post for over a year and although it is too early yet to state what the eventual outcome of the new management arrangements will be, the author's own study in district health authorities was able to point to a number of tensions generated by the imposition of new management strategies.

(i) Increased Centralized Controls
The introduction of general managers in the NHS has pro-

duced a lengthened and more direct chain of hierarchical political control from the Secretary of State for Social Services, through the DHSS, down to regional, district and unit general managers. However it is not yet certain what effect these enhanced political, centralized controls will have on the health service for, as we discuss below, the imposition of general management has created a number of tensions and problems and the new managers have found themselves facing opposition and resistance from the diverse groups within the NHS. Moreover, the Griffiths recommendations have not tackled the conflict between the professional power of the medical practitioners and the management of services at district health authority levels. Doctors are employed by regional health authorities and district general managers have little control over the terms and content of their employment although the introduction of clinical budgeting techniques is an attempt to discipline the medical activities of doctors.

(ii) The Introduction of Clinical Budgeting

A significant element of the Griffiths Report was the introduction of clinical budgeting into medical activity. Professional groups will then have the responsibility of controlling their own resources and costs within the set budget. If managers cannot interfere with the work practices of a profession, setting a budget can act as a form of discipline on the professionals. Attempts by the DHSS to make doctors in particular accountable for their use of resources have been a feature of government reorganizations and rationalizations since the 1960s, and as Dent (1986) has shown the medical profession has until now been able to 'limit the effectiveness of the strategy by attempting to organize an alternative system of self imposed controls on the medical labour process known as the medical audit'. Dent argues that although the individual autonomy of doctors in relation to their work practices has not been affected by managerialist strategies of the DHSS, their institutional autonomy has, that is, the ability of the organized profession collectively to resist the introduction of clinical budgeting. The possibility of allocating scarce life-sustaining resources according to financial criteria can occur under clinical budgeting, absolving the DHSS and health managers from the responsibility of making difficult decisions and from providing extra resources (see also Klein 1983).

The ability of general managers to introduce clinical budgeting as a form of control is however hindered at present by the limited information on medical activities. Integrated computer systems are not yet widespread, although in countries such as Sweden information systems have developed to a point which allows medical activity to be costed (Coombs and Jonsson 1986). When these information systems are developed in Britain, however, it is possible that schemes which operate in the US, such as Diagnostic Related Groups (DRGs) could be implemented (see Chapter 8).

(iii) Increased Gendered Divisions of Labour

The effect of the implementation of the new general management structures has been to widen the already existing gendered divisions of labour in the health service by extending the authority of male managers over nurses. Very few women were appointed to the general manager posts (for example, only 3% of district general managers appointed were women) and many female senior nurses have been made redundant, demoted or have taken early retirement (Hansard 4 March 1986 and 14 March 1986).[3] The predominantly female nursing profession is now excluded from managerial decision-making, as in many districts and units senior nurse managers have been removed from the new management boards and the post of the chief nursing manager with responsibility for nurses has been abolished.[4] Nurses' promotion prospects have also been reduced as they will now have to acquire managerial qualifications and compete for posts as general managers, which may have little to do with the clinical aspects of nursing.

The stratification of nursing labour was, as we saw in Chapter 5, the product of the pursuit of professionalizing strategies of control and closure by nursing elites which created the existing divisions between nurse managers and clinicians, between the qualified and unqualified and between professionalism and unionism. In the 1960s nurse managers were incorporated into management structures, alienating the support and trust of ward-level nurses. Gendered divisions of health labour are therefore crosscut by class divisions within

nursing (Hearn 1982) which have left nurse managers without
a means of calling on the collective support of their own staff
for resistance to changes implemented by the new management arrangements. The Royal College of Nursing has
mounted a national campaign, which drew support in debates
in the House of Commons and the House of Lords, but the
campaign was too late, for general managers were already in
post and the campaign has had little practical impact.

(iv) The Assertion of Managerial Prerogatives

General managers now consider that they have the 'right' to
take decisions on matters that previously were negotiated by
the consensus management team. In many health districts
professional representatives have been removed from the
management board, and the managers now have less opposition to their policies.[5] Evidence from the author's study
suggested further that there was a tendency for managers to
treat the health service as a set of commodities, of plant,
equipment, and manpower, which they had the right to
manage as they saw fit rather than as being held in trust for the
public. This was accompanied by a technocratic rhetoric in
which, for example, hospitals became units of management,
nursing officers became directors of quality assurance, and
people became resource factors. The effect of this was to
objectify labour and the production and nature of health care,
damaging, as we discuss in the next section, the moral commitment of employees to health-care work.

Management's decisions become technical judgements
made on the basis of the most efficient means and least costs,
whilst public debate on the relative importance of the local
health needs of the community were increasingly removed
from the political agenda. This increased technical rationality
and decline of public accountability was aided in several ways
by, for example, a close liaison between politically appointed
chairpersons of health authorities and district general
managers and a much weaker role for health authority
members; lack of public knowledge about the objectives of
the new management boards, or job descriptions of the new
appointments; and lack of consultation, except on a last-
minute basis, of professional groups or unions (interview

notes). To the extent that general managers can convince the public and employees, by their use of language, and by emphasizing technical rationality, that their practices are in the public interest then their scope for further reductions in service and more coercive controls of the labour process are possible but, as discussed below, it is not clear that the managers have yet been successful in legitimating their practices.

Some Emerging Problems

The implementation of general management in the NHS has created tensions, which have undermined and damaged the moral commitment of staff. In the author's own study the undermining of staffs' moral commitment was evident in a number of ways: for some interviewees it was the loss of values of compassion and caring in the service, for others it was reduced public accountability in a service already unresponsive to democratic control, and for others it was the loss of trust and motivation of the lower-level members of the organization.[6] The implementation of specific government policies such as for instance the contracting out of ancillary services, also had the effect of lowering the trust and commitment of staff, and removing the caring contribution that ancillary workers have traditionally made to patient care (see p.177 below). As a consequence, turnover of staff and levels of sickness leave increased, especially amongst nurses and ancillary workers, which threatened the quality, continuity and sometimes even basic provision of health care in the districts[7]. Towards the end of the author's study, managers were beginning to respond to the weakened commitment of employees with a variety of schemes and 'task forces' designed to improve the morale of staff, and to recruit and retain new employees. The imposition of the new managerialism therefore not only exacerbated the tensions between the moral commitment of staff, or the 'collaborative system' as Burns terms it (1981), and the managerial values but was also contradictory in that it undermined the health-care purposes of the health service.

Managers also faced difficulties in legitimating their practices for they were continuously challenged by unions, professional groups and community groups who were able to deny the validity of management ideologies and policies by reference to the social welfare aims of the NHS. Political strategies and the mobilization of public support and opinion were particularly important forms of resistance for health service workers and community groups. Since Mrs Thatcher told the electorate in 1983, that 'the NHS is safe in our hands', the Conservative government has had a political imperative to convince the public and health-service workers that this is indeed the case. The NHS is one of the most popular of state welfare services in Britain and is regarded as an important election issue. The government is therefore under great political pressure to show that its policies are of benefit to all sections of the community, and are orientated to social welfare criteria.

Although the Griffiths Report recognized the management of the NHS as 'an intensely politically sensitive activity', the management principles on which it is based are incompatible with the political pressures to which the government and health managers at both local and national levels are subject. One example is provided by the resignation of the chairman of the NHS Management Board half-way through his term of contract. The chairman stated in his letter of resignation that 'Ministers and the chairman of the management board can approach the same issue with different perspectives, priorities, objectives and restraints. The conclusions are not always compatible' *(Financial Times,* 4 June 1986). The chairman considered that ministerial and political interference had not left him alone to manage the NHS as he wished. His resignation, however, came at a time when the minister was under severe political pressures from the nurses' anti-Griffiths campaign, from public and political anxiety about the under-funding of the service and the effects of RAWP reallocation on prestigious hospitals in London, from the eviction of nurses from nursing homes (an 'efficiency saving') and from political interference in the appointment of health authority chairpersons.

Opposition groups have also been able to use the new managerial structures as a base on which to devise their own responses and resistances. For instance, since general managers have a personal responsibility for decisions taken, local union officials and community health groups now knew 'who their enemy was' (interview notes), and could challenge an individual manager for the consequences of decisions, rather than the anonymous management team that had previously existed. General managers have often found themselves locked in public battles, in the press, on television, in public meetings and in health authorities. In order to survive, general managers have to become politically astute and 'identify areas of mismatch between Griffiths and public accountability, and cultivate micro-political situations' (interview notes). General managers recruited from the private sector have not always been sensitive to the political pressures within the NHS and in some cases, like the chairman, have not survived the full term of their contract.[8]

In conclusion then, the introduction of general management into the health service has, at an early stage, had a number of effects, although the long-term outcomes are as yet uncertain. However the new managerialism has caused considerable disruption, lowering morale and the moral commitment of staff, undermining the effectiveness of patient care, and exacerbating the tensions between managerial values and the 'collaborative' or caring values orientated to the health needs of the population. General managers have found themselves faced with political pressures and oppositions from the diverse groups within the NHS who used the multiple social welfare aims of the NHS to deny the validity of management's claims and practices. The incompatibility between the political imperatives of the NHS and the principles of business management embodied in the Griffiths Report placed sometimes intolerable strains on the general managers, modifying their ability to introduce a new management ethos into the health service. In the longer term the introduction of a market rationality into the NHS may transform the nature of healthcare work, increasing the coercive, authoritarian and patriarchal structures of control. During the transformation period itself, however, it is clear that the tensions and contradictions generated by the new rationality will have unintended consequences which will modify government intentions.

THE CONTRACTING OUT OF ANCILLARY SERVICES IN THE NHS

In 1983 the government issued a circular requiring all health authorities to contract out their catering, laundry and domestic services (DHSS 1983). A few weeks later the government abolished the Fair Wages Resolution of the House of Commons (1946)[9] which meant that private contractors did not have to pay their employees Whitley Council rates of pay and conditions. Since then health authorities have been instructed by ministers not to include fair wages clauses in their contracts.

In its first term of office the government had issued draft circulars on contracting out, but the slow progress of health authorities in this direction brought the government under increasing pressure from a number of groups. First, the UK proponents of the free market, the Adam Smith Institute, Aims of Industry and the CBI, urged the government to privatize, claiming that this was a superior form of service provision (for example, Forsyth 1982, CBI 1981). Second, in 1982, the Institute of Directors published a paper which advocated privatization as 'the obvious and most desirable' strategy of breaking the strength of the public sector unions, by reducing union membership and making bargaining arrangements more localized (Institute of Directors 1982). Third, the contracting companies themselves considered that contracting out in the NHS would provide them with ready and profitable markets, around £175 million a year according to the PR firm of Forsyth (*The Guardian,* 5 July 1984). Fourth, pressure also came from a parliamentary lobby consisting of some thirty MPs who had shares in the private companies or who were directors or consultants to the firms (Tribune 1985). Fifth, contracting out was an attractive policy to a government committed to reducing public expenditure and public employment and weakening the strength of the public sector unions which were considered to be outside the market discipline which by then had affected the private sector unions (see Chapter 6). Lastly, professional legitimation had also come earlier from public administration associations (Dunleavy 1986).

Hence the political compulsion for health authorities to contract out, despite the lack of evidence that contracting out is cheaper in the long term than the direct production of services. In some cases health authorities have been instructed to award contracts to private companies even when their own in-house bids have been lower (Labour Research May 1984).

The government claim that the policy of contracting out is part of its aim of achieving the 'best value for money in the NHS and the maximum amount of resources devoted to patient care'. However, to date the amount of money saved by contracting out has only been a very small proportion of the total NHS revenue allocation. For example, by September 1986 the government claimed that two-thirds of ancillary services had been put out to tender at a 'saving' of £73 million. These 'savings' represented 0.8% of the total NHS budget, and since private contractors had won only 18% of the contracts at this time, their contribution was only around 0.3% of the budget (Hansard, 25th November 1986).[10] Moreover cash 'savings' achieved through contracting out generate increased public expenditure through hidden administrative costs, increased monitoring and evaluation costs, through contractors' failures and cost overruns, as well as increased costs to other public agencies through redundancies and increased unemployment. Social costs are also generated which are borne by health workers, whose pay and conditions are reduced, and by patients through reduced levels and quality of service. Women in particular bear the brunt of these costs as ancillary workers and as the main users of the services (Radical Statistics Health Group 1987).

Management Strategies

As we have seen in section one of this chapter, general managers were appointed on short-term contracts to make 'major improvements in savings', and their future careers and possible salary levels depend on showing that they have succeeeded in this respect.[11] Privatization of ancillary services was one area where they could make changes without affecting front-line staff or closing hospitals. Ancillary workers tend to be an 'invisible' element of hospital workers; unlike nurses they are not 'public figures' so that the contracting out of ancillary services was less likely to become a local public issue than closing hospitals, wards or beds.

Nevertheless, general managers disliked the political compulsion and political dogma behind the tendering process; they disliked the loss of control over their own staff, the loss of trust and commitment of ancillary managers and workers, and the breakup of the ancillary team. As the tendering programme progressed it became clear that there were also associated problems of maintaining standards and monitoring the contracts, especially when contractors failed to provide an adequate service.

These conflicting pressures on management could, however, be reconciled by winning the in-house tender, but to win management had to undercut the unknown bids of the contractors. Data obtained from the DHSS by Frank Dobson MP shows that there is a trend for more and more contracts to be won by in-house tenders (Hansard 14 April 1986).[12] The tendering programme has proceeded more rapidly for domestic services, for as they are more labour-intensive than either laundry or catering there is a greater margin of cost reduction or profits for private companies.

Union Strategies
The trade unions are also caught in a dilemma, for if they negotiate with management during the preparation of the in-house tender they may be agreeing to a deterioration of pay and conditions of work for their members which, if the in-house tender wins, may be worse than the conditions of private contractors. If the contractors win they are likely to lose members and negotiating rights and their members may lose jobs, or suffer loss of pay and reduced terms and conditions of work. The fragmented and decentralized nature of contracting out, and management control of the contracting process, has meant that union leaders are at a loss as to know how to deal directly with privatization. At a local level, there have been examples of successful struggles by unions who have been able to prevent the lowering of wages and conditions of ancillary workers in certain districts. But sectionalism between the different unionized and professional groups

within the NHS has, however, hindered the ancillaries from gaining substantial support.

A further problem for the unions is the low public visibility of ancillary workers, for privatization of ancillary work generated, as mentioned above, little local attention. As was argued in section one of this chapter though, the most successful strategy for the unions at a national level has been that which utilizes the widespread public support for the NHS. The unions' national anti-privatization publicity campaigns, for instance, have helped to prevent the widespread privatization of the NHS which was promised in the earlier years of the Conservative administration.

Labour Relations During the Tendering Process

At the time of writing there have been only a small number of studies of labour relations during the tendering process, but those that are available show a wide variety of management responses to contracting out and the involvement of unions (Leedham 1986, Mailly 1986 and the author's own research). In some districts unions have been involved in negotiating both the specifications and tendering process, in others unions have been consulted during these processes. In a number of districts, however, unions have been excluded altogether as management has attempted to gain the co-operation of the workforce more directly. These responses reflect the different strengths of local unions, the extent of inter-union co-operation and forms of accommodation between management and unions, which are themselves a product of the local history of labour relations in the district.[13] The political balance of the health authority members, and the particular management styles and strategies adopted by district management, are also important in determining the extent of union involvement[14] (Mailly 1986, Leedham 1986).

In most districts the specifications and in-house tender have been perceived as a managerial activity with a dominant influence from work study officers. Mailly indicates in his study that there was little union input into the specifications, as the inexperience of local officers led them to underestimate the importance of this stage of the process. Management was therefore able to control the numbers of staff, wage levels, conditions of work, hours of work, and work routines implied by the specifications.[15]

During the contracting-out process the studies indicate that labour relations were likely to be more acrimonious and adverse, although this was also produced by the new style adopted by general managers. In this context contracting out was only one aspect of the changing frontiers of control in the public welfare sector. Leedham found that local relations were soured whatever the outcome of contracting out and, recognizing this, management felt able to confront the unions and tackle other contentious issues that previously would have been unchallenged in the name of good relations (1986).

Costs to Ancillary Workers

Since ancillary services are labour-intensive, costs can only be reduced by intensifying work and lowering the wages and working conditions of staff. This applies to contracts won by in-house tenders as much as those won by private contractors. As London Health Emergency has said, for ancillary workers the choice is 'heads they win—tails you lose' (London Health Emergency 1986). The costs of contracting out are, therefore borne by ancillary workers who suffer redundancies, reduced pay, reduced conditions of work, loss of bonus payments, loss of overtime and shift payments, excessive use of part-time work, increased workloads, and reduced access to union protection, although grave abuses of these are more prevalent in the private companies (NUPE/SCAT 1985). Contracting out therefore restructures the labour force within the health service, segmenting different groups by their terms and conditions of employment into core and casualized forms of labour.

Ancillary work is predominantly work done by women (67% of ancillary staff are women), and in some parts of the country ethnic minority workers. Women ancillary workers are concentrated in Grades 1-3 of the NHS pay scale, earning between £72-£75 a week in 1985-1986. The trade unions argue that 80% of female ancillary workers earn less than 'official' levels (that is, supplementary benefit levels) of poverty (Ancillary Staffs Council Trade Union Side 1985). So even before a service is contracted out, ancillary workers are amongst the lowest-paid groups in the country. Like the introduction of general management, contracting out also reshapes gender relations within the health service, marginalizing and making more insecure the forms of work carried out by women.

The Contract-in Operation

If a private contractor wins the contract, the work of the ancillaries becomes commodified, both cheapened and conducted for profit; the labour process is now subject to the discipline of market criteria. If an in-house tender wins, however, the service has still been subjected to the discipline of competition and although labour is not conducted for the extraction of profit, the labour process is organized as if it were. During the tendering process itself organization of the labour process can be changed to make it more competitive by introducing labour-saving equipment, employing casual and part-time staff, leaving vacancies unfilled, reviewing and tightening bonus schemes, and conducting 'efficiency reviews'. Moreover, the theory behind competitive tendering is that competition is continuous; as the contract is only for a limited duration competition must extend through the life of the contract. The contractor cannot become complacent; managers and workers are now under an obligation to keep to the terms of the contract, which must be continuously monitored and evaluated.

The process of tendering also has the effect of lowering the trust and morale of staff, so that even if an in-house tender wins a contract, the commitment of health workers to health care and patient-orientated tasks is damaged or undermined. If a private contractor wins a tender, the experience and dedication of the workforce built up over many years is lost as the ancillary team is broken up. Ancillary managers are made redundant or are taken on as monitoring officers with no career prospects or pay progression. The basis of compliance is weakened since managers can no longer make moral appeals to staff on the grounds of the hospital team or identity with the hospital, although winning the in-house tender has been used by management as a source of pride and motivation (*Health Service Journal* 24 April 1986). Since the contract is only for a short duration, the staff also feel continuously under threat and insecure.

Once a contract is in operation it becomes socially divisive for the health workers, irrespective of whether it is in-house or private. As we saw above, the labour force becomes segmented, as conditions of work and terms of employment are casualized. In addition, ancillary workers are no longer part of the health-care team, but become isolated and separated by the factory-like regime of work which conflicts with the patient care values and priorities of other health-care workers. The intensification of work means that ancillary workers can no longer make the traditional caring contribution to patient care which the work process of direct labour allowed. The workloads of nurses are also intensified as they have to take on patient-orientated tasks previously carried out by ancillaries, and through the additional domestic work which the ancillary workers cannot do in the times allowed.[16] The different regime of work imposed by the contract can also be incompatible with other welfare policies, for example, in the author's study, the routinized and intensified nature of contract ancillary work reduced the effectiveness of the flexibility of domestic work required by the rehabilitation programmes of community care.[17]

As argued earlier, however, control of the labour process is a continuously contested and negotiated process. There is no one panacea for management control structures which once imposed means that all resistance has been quelled. Rather the variable dimension of labour power remains with workers and management are still dependent on the subjective input of labour. Private contractors and health authorities working to an in-house contract have already experienced difficulties in recruiting staff as well as rapid turnover of staff, and this is exacerbated in areas where there are similar but higher-paid jobs and higher costs of living, such as London and the southeast of England.[18] As a consequence there are problems in retaining and training staff, and continuity and quality of service have been reduced (Public Service Action, 22, 1986).

Like the bonus schemes, the contract also codifies rules and procedures giving workers and the unions some leverage within the contract; for example, in the author's study, the contract was used by staff to enforce the authorities' duties and responsibilities. Staff also used the contract as a set of rules which stipulated minimum performance. Since workloads were intensified and times for work tasks reduced, the ancillary workers' attitude was 'if standards are not achieved in the time set, that is a management problem'. The intensification of work, a weakened moral commitment and minimum compliance with the contract are undoubtedly factors which contribute to the high failure rate of the private contracts.

Even for an in-house tender, however, contracts can be more inflexible than direct labour, and overruns on budgets can increase costs to health authorities. The nature of healthcare work means that it is difficult to include all contingencies of ancillary work in the specifications; accidents and emergencies, for instance, are unpredictable. Ancillary managers also recognize that for certain patients there will always be additional but unpredictable amounts of work, but as these are outside routine work they cannot be costed or included in work study data.

In conclusion, this discussion of contracting out in the NHS has attempted to examine the conflicting pressures operating on local health managers and trade unionists when faced with the political compulsion to implement a policy which they perceived as inappropriate or illegitimate. Whilst the terms of contract of the new general managers have been a means of ensuring that the policy is complied with, the managers have attempted to resolve its inherent problems by winning the in-house tender. They have, however, used the contracting-out programme as a means of asserting managerial prerogatives in labour relations in ways which are consistent with the principles of general management. At a national level unions have found that political strategies have been the best means of opposing privatization.

Early studies have shown that contracting out in the NHS has restructured the ancillary labour process. The labour force has become more segmented as casualized or marginalized forms of contract labour have been introduced, and ancillary workers have become separated from other healthcare workers by the different regime of work imposed by the contract. Contracting out has not only produced changes in the relations of production for the contract workers, but has also reshaped gender relations by reducing the terms, conditions and security of a form of work predominantly carried out by women.

However, although contracting out imposes more coercive forms of control on ancillary workers, they have engaged in forms of passive resistance, creating a number of problems for management which have damaged and reduced the levels, quality and continuity of health care. Management now has no basis on which to elicit the compliance of staff, since their trust and morale has been lowered, and managers have to find new ways of increasing moral commitment and efforts of staff. Managers also face difficulties in recruiting, retaining and training staff for their in-house contracts in ways which do not conflict with patient care. Moreover, contracting out shifts the problems of managing and providing a service to those of monitoring, supervising and evaluating the contract, of cost overruns and of providing emergency measures to secure continuity of care when contractors fail to provide adequate services.

NOTES

1. The research was carried out by means of fifty semi-structured interviews with general managers, trade union branch officials, and employees in two district health authorities, and by analysis of published and unpublished documents, during the period October 1985 to April 1986. NHS managers and staff were interviewed in acute hospitals, pyschiatric and mentally-handicapped hospitals and in community services in the two districts. The research study was funded by the School of Business and Social Sciences, Hatfield Polytechnic.
2. Of the 744 general managers, 60% were previously administrators, 15% were doctors, and 9% were nurses (Hansard 26 June 1986).
3. 6 out of 180 district general managers were women. At the time of writing, information available for 9 out of the 14 health regions showed that 60 out of 359 unit general managers (17%) were women (*Health Service Journal* 1986).
4. An RCN survey of 150 district health authorities found that twenty-eight districts had removed the chief nursing officer post and there was no nurse member of the management team. In fifty-seven other

districts hybrid posts had been created so that although the chief nursing officer role is retained they have additional responsibilities for services such as ancillary services or ambulances. In nine of these districts there is a CNO who is advisory and again excluded from the management board; in forty-six districts the chief nursing officer is both advisor for all nursing in the district and has responsibility for all nurse education in the district. At unit level, senior nursing managers have now to report to a general manager rather than to a district nursing officer and in many units the senior management posts have been removed. (Hansard 14 March 1986, p.1368; also Action Pack on Griffiths, RCN, January 1986).

5.   The assertion of managerial prerogatives was attempted through increased disciplining of staff, an emphasis on contractual obligations and the pushing through of government policies such as privatization and 'efficiency savings', which in some areas has meant the closure of hospitals, wards or beds. In industrial relations, managers showed a new willingness to confront union leaders, and adopted an adversarial stance, often dishonouring earlier industrial relations agreements.

6.   The author's study found heightened insecurity and uncertainty amongst staff, especially middle management and senior nurses, as well as more intrumental attitudes, lack of motivation, and minimum adherence to rules. An increase in sectionalism between the different groups and an emphasis on self or occupational interests were also evident.

7.   At a national level the high turnover of nurses has given serious concern; see for example the Committee of Public Accounts, 14th Report, 1985-1986: *The Control of Nursing Manpower*.

8.   At the time of writing four district general managers recruited from outside the health service had resigned in mid-contract because of 'political' interference in the management function by the health authorities.

9.   The House of Commons Fair Wages Resolution of 1946 instructed government departments to require contractors to provide their workers with terms and conditions 'not less favourable than those established for the trade or industry in the district where the work is carried out' (Heald and Morris 1984, p.31)

10.   Private contractors have experienced a number of problems in the tendering programme: lack of success in winning tenders and therefore less profits than initially anticipated; termination of some contracts in mid-term; financial difficulties of some companies; and the withdrawal of others from the tendering programme altogether (London Health Emergency 1986). These difficulties have led the contractors association (The Contract Cleaning and Maintenance Association) to put pressure on the government to change the rules of contracting out in their favour. Accordingly in January 1986 new instructions which do favour the contractors were issued to health authorities by the DHSS. The rules include advice to health districts not to investigate the projected workloads or the terms and conditions

of service for employees, nor the expected profit margins of contractors; the rules have also made it more difficult for districts to terminate a contract when companies fail to provide an adequate service (DHSS 1985).

11. In a report written by the accounting firm of Coopers and Lybrand (1985), appointed by the government to find ways of making contracting out more attractive for the contractors, it is considered that the initial phase of the tendering process was constrained by the former consensus management teams which handled the process on a 'committee type basis'. General managers, however, have brought a much more 'incisive approach', which the report considers has greater potential for the contractors in the second generation of contracting out.

12. Between May and November 1985, 78% of cleaning contracts had been won in-house; between November 1985 and April 1986, 85% of cleaning contracts had been won in-house (Hansard 14 April 1986).

13. In the study conducted by the author, labour relations in one district were characterized by strong inter-union co-operation and organization, high union density and 'traditional' understandings with management established during the consensus period of the 1970s. Management adopted a strategy of non-confrontation with the unions, who were able to participate in the preparation of the specifications and in-house tender. The unions were given full information, were able to use delaying tactics, and to assess the contractors invited to tender. For management however it was a successful strategy, for union branch officers persuaded their members to relinquish their bonuses and accept a reduction in pay and conditions. The in-house tender won and union officers felt that at least they had preserved jobs and NHS negotiating procedures.

In another district, unions (who did not have inter-union organization) were consulted in the preparation of the in-house tender, but they and their members wished to keep their bonus payments and Whitley conditions of work and pay. Management considered that it was under pressure from the minister to exclude fair-wages clauses from the contracts, and ignored the preferences of the unions and the workforce. The in-house tender won but employees and branch officials were demoralized, and lack of trust in district management became a characteristic of subsequent labour relations.

14. For example, health authorities which were much quicker to tender and had contracted a larger proportion of their services at the time of writing are in the south-east of England where Conservative voters predominate, but not in inner London where the Labour party is more dominant and the public sector a major employer (Public Service Action No. 21 1986).

15. The specifications stipulated the levels, frequencies and standards of service required. Although they could not specify employment levels, they did determine numbers of staff, wage levels, conditions of work, hours of work, and work routines.

16. A National Audit Office Report on Nursing Manpower found that nurses now spend a considerable proportion (21%) of their time on catering and domestic duties (Committee of Public Accounts 14th Report 1985-1986).
17. Nurses working on the rehabilitation of mentally ill or mentally handicapped patients taught patients everyday domestic activities such as cooking, cleaning and washing before they left to live in community homes. The flexibility of domestic, catering and laundry work required by this rehabilitation programme conflicted however with the rigid and routinized schedules of contract ancillary work.
18. In Croydon DHA, for example, in the first five months of a cleaning contract by Crothalls, 87 people held 25 jobs (*The Guardian*, 13 March 1986).

Conclusion

It has been stressed throughout this book that state work is ambiguous and contradictory, external to yet dependent on the capital-wage-labour relation. Clearly, though, there are a number of ways in which state workers, as wage workers, have similar work processes and terms and conditions of work to their counterparts in the private sector. Hence 'Although state workers are not directly exploited by capital, their experience of unemployment, wage pressure and deskilling etc, is very much as a result of their insertion into a capitalist economy' (Meiksins 1986, p.113).

Moreover, as we have discussed in the previous chapters, the introduction of technical and market rationalities into state organizations has created pressures of bureaucratization and intensification of work which, as both Weber and Braverman identified, are as coercive as those in private sector organizations. State welfare organizations therefore have, as we noted, a 'factory like' logic. Forms of social inequalities are perpetuated and developed for both workers and clients, for instance the persistence of high concentrations of low-paid jobs, gendered and racial divisions of labour, and forms of stigmatism and dependency induced by professional and bureaucratic definitions of clients' 'needs'.

Nevertheless we have also argued, following the ideas of the critical theorists Habermas and Offe, that state production as well as reproducing capitalist social relations also introduces new and additional forms of social relations which negate the capital-labour relation. Thus for example welfare services are produced according to criteria other than

exchange values. These services also provide a material resource for labour that mitigates to some extent the exploitative relation of capital and labour, especially for women and
ethnic minority groups. The state sector can provide progressive employment and labour relations practices—for instance
equal opportunity practices, contract compliance policies, or
health and safety procedures—practices which advance the
public interest although these may not be the agencies'
specific policy objectives (see Dunleavy 1986).

The state's production of welfare is also opened to public
debate and the nature and distribution of these services
becomes contested, an arena of conflict and struggle. To the
extent that these forms of action increased the financial and
political problems of the state, the state responded with more
repressive mechanisms of control, directed to state workers,
unions and clients, as well as measures of confinement and
control directed to the civil society.

It has been argued in the preceding chapters that the
theories of the critical theorists provided a model with which
to analyse the relation of the internal organization of state
welfare to wider economic and political changes. In particular
the notion that the state sector is governed by a different
mode of rationality from that which governs the private sector
has proved useful in understanding managerial strategies,
labour relations, divisions of labour and changes in work
organization in state welfare organizations. Thus we have
been able to analyse the particular difficulties state managers
face in formulating appropriate strategies of control in organizations governed by non-market criteria but which are
dependent for their resources on capitalist production. We
have also been able to examine the contradictory effects of
non-commensurate policies and their implications for the
organization and control of welfare work.

The previous chapters have traced the attempts by the state
to contain costs in the labour-intensive welfare services, either
through incomes policies, industrial relations policies or
rationalizations and reorganizations of work. But in the 1970s
these policies contributed to the rising relative costs of state
welfare through increasing bureaucratization and through
wage rises gained as a result of militant action by the public

sector unions. The greater strength and organization of the public sector unions has enabled them to resist, especially at a local level, subsequent government policies directed against welfare production. But public union action and militancy also heightened a climate of opinion in which state workers and the state-dependent population are seen as unproductive burdens on wealth creation. The 'special conditions of exchange' of state welfare workers therefore implicated them in the financial and political problems of governments in the 1970s, which contributed to the conditions in which the influence of the ideas of the new right took root in the political realignments of this period.

Recent attempts to restructure state welfare work have arisen therefore through the structural location of the state as well as specific political and ideological practices. Recent policies directed to welfare work have included attempts to reduce state expenditure and employment and introduce forms of technical and market criteria and rationality into welfare organizations. But such measures have also generated further financial and social costs for the state, have tended to undermine and obscure the purposes of state welfare work, and have produced a number of tensions and problems for state managers, which have further to be resolved.

Issues of legitimacy and the requirement that governments respond to political pressures constitute, to use Batstone's term, 'political contingencies' which affect the strategies adopted by both state managers and workers. Political strategies (as well as industrial action) have therefore been an important resource which trade unions and other opposition groups have used to deny the validity of management's practices and ideologies. However, as we discussed in Chapter 6, differences between the labour movements in the US and the UK have affected the conditions in which public services and employment were expanded in the two countries, and therefore the political resources and support which the public unions can draw on in each country.

The restructuring of welfare work is only one aspect of the restructuring of industry and of the labour force that has taken place in recent years in the US, the UK, and other market economies. This restructuring has to be understood in terms of the national and international relocation of capital, employers' practices, and government policies. Evidence from both the US and the UK shows a decline of male, manual and unionized jobs in manufacturing industries and a growth in the low-waged, feminized and non-unionized service industries. In the state welfare sector there has also been a growth of low-waged and predominantly part-time feminized jobs, so that women workers can now be said to be a permanent part of the workforce rather than its most disposable part. As we discussed in Chapter 4, employers also organize their workforce in gender-specific ways, since many of the jobs that women do in the public services are domestic and unqualified caring jobs that draw on skills women learn informally in the home.

In the labour force generally there has been further segmentation through attempts to create both a casualized and marginal labour force more exposed to the direct effects of economic constraints and a core workforce attached to the firm through various employment packages. In the public sector the government has also attempted to create similar divisions through the introduction of such strategies as contracting out and forms of market criteria in the organization of welfare services. In the NHS in Britain the contracting out of ancillary services has led to more casualized forms of labour as contract labour has been introduced, and these workers have become separated from other welfare workers by the different regime of work imposed by the contract. But these policies have had the effect of undermining and damaging the moral commitment and caring work on which managers of state welfare provision are dependent.

In the private sector employers are seeking to co-opt key workers on the basis of a new commitment and through new motivational mechanisms; in the public sector, government policies for its own workforce have undermined the motivation and commitment of that workforce. Similarly, in the US the new 'supply-side' managers in public administration have emerged at a time when participatory management and Japanese-style labour-management relations are current in many private companies (Caroll *et al.* 1985). As Brown (1986) has commented: 'The public services trauma of the 1980s is thus not just one of financial crisis but of a challenge to a whole system of labour control and motivation' (p.167).

Opposition to government's attack on welfare has been impeded by ideologies of professionalism which, as we have seen, prevents alliances and works as a preventative against the unity of welfare workers. Resistance has also been hindered by conflicts of economic and ideological interests between state and private sector workers, which have further fragmented class interests already segmented along labour market, gender and ethnic lines. The shared interests of state workers and private sector workers are thus obscured by the divisions and conflicts of interests between them, especially in the US where a greater degree of anti-statism exists. Common interests are however also concealed by ideologies of the right which stress the public sector as a burden and parasitic growth on the private sector, and by forms of technical rationality which depoliticize the state's activities.

Bibliography

N. Abercrombie and J. Urry (1983) *Capital, Labour and the Middle Classes*, George Allen and Unwin, London; Allen and Unwin Inc. Winchester Mass.

P. Abrams (1982) *Historical Sociology*, Open Books, Pitman Press, Bath.

M. Albrow (1970) *Bureaucracy*, Pall Mall Press, London.

V. L. Allen (1975) *Social Analaysis: A Marxist Critique and Alternative*, Longman, London.

Ancillary Staffs Council Trade Union Side (1985) 'Health Workers' Pay: Time for Action Now', November.

D. Armstrong (1976) 'The Decline of Medical Hegemony: A Review of Government Reports During the NHS', *Social Service and Medicine*, 10 Part 3/4 pp.157-63.

J. Atkinson (1985) 'Is the Secondary Market Here to Stay?', *Employment Bulletin and IR Digest*, June.

R. Bacon and W. Eltis (1976) *Britain's Economic Problem: Too Few Producers*, Macmillan, London.

M. Barrett (1980) *Women's Oppression Today: Problems in Marxist Feminist Analysis*, Verso, London.

M. Barrett and M. McIntosh (1980) 'The Family Wage: Some Problems for Socialists and Feminists', *Capital and Class*, 11.

E. Batstone, A. Ferner, and M. Terry (1984) *Consent and Efficiency: Labour Relations and Management Strategy in the State Enterprise*, Basil Blackwell, Oxford.

P. B. Beaumont (1982) 'Strikes and the Public Sector: The Position in Britain', *Employee Relations*, 4 No. 2, pp.23-7.

V. Beechey (1977) 'Some Notes on Female Wage Labour in Capitalist Production, *Capital and Class*, 3, pp.45-66.

V. Beechey (1978) 'Women and Production: A Critical Analysis of some Sociological Theories of Women's Work', in A. Kuhn and A. M. Wolpe (Eds.) (1978) *Feminism and Materialism,* Routledge and Kegan Paul, London.

V. Beechey (1982) 'The Sexual Division of Labour and the Labour Process: A Critical Assessment of Braverman', in S. Wood (Ed.) (1982) *The Degradation of Work? Skill, Deskilling and the Labour Process,* Hutchinson, London.

V. Beechey (1984) 'Women and Employment', Open University U221, *The Changing Experience of Women,* Unit 11, The Open University Press, Milton Keynes.

V. Beechey and T. Perkins (1985) 'Conceptualising Part Time Work', in B. Roberts, Ruth Finnegan and D. Gallie (Eds.) (1985) *New Approaches to Economic Life,* Manchester University Press, Manchester.

D. Bell (1973) *The Coming of Post Industrial Society,* Heinemann, London.

D. E. Bell (1985) 'Unionized Women in State and Local Government', in R. Milkman (Ed.) *Women, Work and Protest: A Century of Women's Labour History,* Routledge and Kegan Paul, Boston and London.

P. Bellaby and P. Oribabar (1980) 'Determinants of Occupational Strategies Adopted by British Hospital Nurses' *International Journal of Health Services,* 10, No. 2, pp.291-309.

J. K. Benson (1981) 'Organizations : A Dialectical View', in M. Zey-Ferrell and M. Aiken *Complex Organizations: Critical Perspectives,* Scott, Foresman and Co., Illinois.

P. L. Berger and T. Luckman (1966) *The Social Construction of Reality,* Allen Lane, London.

E. Bittner (1965) 'The Concept of Organization', *Social Research,* 32, No. 3.

P. Blau (1963) *The Dynamics of Bureaucracy,* University of Chicago Press, Chicago.

P. Blau (1970) 'Weber's Theory of Bureaucracy', in D. Wrong (Ed.) *Max Weber,* Prentice Hall, Englewood Cliffs, NJ.

P. Blau and R. W. Scott (1963 *Formal Organizations: A Comparative Approach,* Routledge and Kegan Paul, London.

P. Boreham (1983) 'Indetermination, Professional Knowledge, Organization and Control', *The Sociological Review,* 31, No. 4, pp.693-718.

N. Bosenquet (1983) *After The New Right,* Heinemann, London.

H. Braverman (1974) 'Labor and Monopoly Capital', *Monthly Review Press,* New York.

I. Breugal (1979) 'Women as a Reserve Army: A Note on Recent British Experience', *Feminist Review,* 3, pp.12-23.

D. Brody (1980) *Workers in Industrial America: Essays on the Twentieth-Century Struggle,* Oxford University Press, New York.

W. Brown (1986) 'The Changing Role of Trade Unions in the Management of Labour', *British Journal of Industrial Relations,* 24, No. 2, July, pp.161-8.

J. Buchanan and R. E. Wagner (1977) *Democracy in Deficit: the Political Legacy of Lord Keynes,* Academic Press, New York.

M. Burawoy (1979) *Manufacturing Consent,* Chicago University Press, Chicago.

M. Burawoy (1985) *The Politics of Production: Factory Regimes Under Capitalism and Socialism,* Verso, London.

T. Burns (1981) 'A Comparative Study of Administrative Structure and Organizational Processes in Selected Areas of the NHS', SSRC Research Report.

T. Burns and G. M. Stalker (1961) *The Management of Innovation,* Tavistock, London.

G. Burrell (1986) 'Fragmented Labour': paper presented to the Fourth Annual Aston/UMIST Conference on the Organization and Control of the Labour Process.

G. Burrell and G. Morgan (1979) *Sociological Paradigms and Organizational Analysis,* Heinemann, London.

G. Carchedi (1977) *On The Economic Identification of Social Classes,* Routledge and Kegan Paul, London.

M. Carpenter (1976) 'The New Managerialism and Professionalism in Nursing', in M. Stacey *et al.* (Eds.) *Health and the Division of Labour,* Croom Helm, London.

M. Carpenter (1982) 'The Labour Movement in the NHS', in A. S. Sethi and S. Dimmock (Eds.) (1982) *Industrial Relations and Health Services,* Croom Helm, London.

A. M. Carr-Saunders and P. A. Wilson (1964) *The Professions,* Frank Cass, London.

J. Carrier and I. Kendall (1986) 'NHS Management and the Griffiths Report', in *Year Book of Social Policy in Britain 1985/6,* Routledge and Kegan Paul, London.

J. D. Carroll, A. L. Fritschler and B. L. R. Smith (1985) 'Supply Side Management in the Reagan Administration', *Public Administration Review,* November/December, pp.805-14.

S. Castles and G. Kosack (1973) *Immigrant Workers and the Class Structure,* Oxford University Press and the Institute of Race Relations, London.

A. Cawson (1982) *Corporatism and Welfare,* Heinemann, London.

A. Cawson and P. Saunders (1983) 'Corporatism and Competitive Politics and Class Struggle, in R. King (Ed.) *Capital and Politics,*

Routledge and Kegan Paul, London.

J. Child (1972) 'Organizational Structure, Environment and Performance: The Role of Strategic Choice' *Sociology*, 6, No. 1, January.

J. Child (1984) 'New Technology and the Service Class': Working Paper, Work Organization Research Unit, Aston University, Birmingham.

J. Child (1985) 'Managerial Strategies, New Technology and the Labour Process', in D. Knights, H. Willmott and D. Collinson (Eds.) *Job Redesign: Critical Perspectives on the Labour Process*, Gower, Aldershot, Hants.

S. Clegg and D. Dunkerley (1980) *Organization, Class and Control*, Routledge and Kegan Paul, London.

C. Cockburn (1983) *Brothers: Male Dominance and Technological Change*, Pluto Press, London.

Confederation of British Industry (1981), *Report of CBI Working Party on Government Expenditure*, London.

R. Coombs (1978) 'Labor and Monopoly Capital', *New Left Review*, 107.

R. Coombs (1985) 'Automation, Management Strategies and Labour Process Change', in D. Knights, H. Willmott and D. Collinson (Eds.) *Job Redesign: Critical Perspectives on the Labour Process*, Gower, Aldershot, Hants.

R. V. Coombs and O. Jonsson (1986) 'New Technology and Management in a Non-Market Environment': paper presented to the Fourth Aston/UMIST Annual Conference on the Organization and Control of the Labour Process.

Coopers and Lybrand Associates (1986) 'Health Management Update File'.

C. Cousins (1986) 'The Labour Process in the State Welfare Sector'. in D. Knights and H. Willmott (Eds.) *Managing the Labour Process*, Gower.

A. Coyle (1984) *Redundant Women*, The Women's Press, London.

P. Cressey and J. McInnes (1980) 'Industrial Democracy and the Control of Labour', *Capital and Class*, 11.

R. Crompton and J. Gubbay (1977) *Economy and Class Structure*, Macmillan, London.

R. Crompton and G. Jones (1984) *White Collar Proletariat: Deskilling and Gender in Clerical Work*, Macmillian, London.

C. Crouch (1979) *The Politics of Industrial Relations*, Fontana Books, London.

M. Crozier (1964) *The Bureaucratic Phenomenon*, Tavistock, London; University of Chicago, Chicago.

M. Crozier (1975) *The Crisis of Democracy: Report on the Govern-*

ability of Democracies to the Trilateral Commission, New York University Press, New York.

CSE Sex and Class Group (1982) 'Sex and Class', *Capital and Class.* 16, pp.78-94.

CSE State Group (1979) *Struggle Over the State: Cuts and Restructuring in Contemporary Britain*, CSE Books, London.

D. E. Cullen (1985) 'Recent Trends in Collective Bargaining in the United States', *International Labor Review*, 124, No. 3.

J. Dale and P. Foster (1986), *Feminists and State Welfare*, Routledge and Kegan Paul, London and Boston.

C. Davies and J. Rosser (1984) 'Gendered Jobs in the Health Service: A Problem for Labour Process Analysis': paper presented to the Second Aston/UMIST Annual Conference on the Organization and Control of the Labour Process.

M. Davis (1982) 'The AFL—CIO's Second Century', *New Left Review*, 136.

M. Davis (1984a) 'The Political Economy of Late Imperial America', *New Left Review*, 143.

M. Davis (1984b) 'The New Right's Road to Power', *New Left Review*, 148.

R. Day and J. V. Day (1977) 'A Review of the Current State of Negotiated Order Theory: An Appreciation and a Critique', *Sociological Quarterly*, 18, pp.126-42.

M. Dent (1986) 'Autonomy and the Medical Profession: Medical Audit and Management Control': paper presented to the Fourth Aston/UMIST Annual Conference on the Organization and Control of the Labour Process.

C. Derber (1982) *Professionals as Workers: Mental Labor in Advanced Capitalism*, G. K. Hall, Boston.

C. Derber (1983) 'Managing Professionals: Ideological Proletarianization and Post Industrial Labor', *Theory and Society*, 12, pp.309-41.

C. Derber (1984) 'Sponsorship and Control of Physicians', in J. B. McKinley (Ed.) *Issues in the Political Economy of Health Care*, Tavistock, London and New York.

S. Dex (1985) *The Sexual Division of Work: Conceptual Revolutions in the Social Sciences*, Wheatsheaf Books, Brighton.

S. Dex and S. M. Perry (1984) 'Women's Employment Changes in the 1970's, *Employment Gazette*, April, pp.151-64.

DHSS (1976a) 'Sharing Resources for Health in England', HMSO, London.

DHSS (1976b) 'Priorities for Health and Personal Social Services in England', HMSO, London.

DHSS (1983) Circular HS(83) 18, September.

DHSS (1985) 'Competitive Tendering: Further Advice for Health Authorities', December, HMSO, London.

DHSS (1986) 'General Managers: Arrangements for Remuneration and Conditions of Service', May.

P. B. Doeringer and M. J. Piore (1971) *Internal Labour Markets and Manpower Analysis*, D. C. Heath, Lexington, Mass.

I. Douglas and S. Lord (1986) *Local Government Finance: A Practical Guide*, The Local Government Information Unit, London.

A. Downs (1957) *Inside Bureaucracy*, Little Brown, Boston.

L. Doyal (1983) 'Women, Health and the Sexual Division of Labour: A Case Study of the Women's Health Movement in Britain', *International Journal of Health Services*, 13, No. 3.

L. Doyal, G. Hunt and J. Mellor (1981) 'Your Life in their Hands: Migrant Workers in the NHS', *Critical Social Policy*, 1, No. 2.

P. Draper and T. Smart (1974) 'Social Science and Health Policy in the UK: Some Contributions of the Social Sciences to the Bureaucratization of the NHS', *International Journal of Health Services*, 4 No. 3, pp.453-70.

R. Dredge (1983) 'American Revolution Over the Rising Hospital Bill', *Health and Social Service Journal*, 3 (November) pp.1316-17.

P. Dunleavy (1980a) 'The Political Implications of Sectoral Cleavages and the Growth of State Employment: Part I The Analysis of Production Cleavages', *Political Studies*, 28, pp.364-83.

P. Dunleavy (1980b), 'The Political Implications of Sectoral Cleavages and the Growth of State, Employment: Part II Cleavage Structure and Political Alignment',· *Political Studies*, 28, pp.527-49.

P. Dunleavy (1986) 'Explaining the Privatization Boom: Public Choice versus Radical Approaches', *Public Administration*, 64, Spring, pp.13-34.

Economic Trends (February 1983) No. 352, 'Employment in the Public and Private Sectors, 1976-1982'.

Economic Trends (March 1985) No. 377. 'Employment in the Public and Private Sectors 1978-1984.

P. K. Edwards (1981) *Strikes in the United States 1881-1974*, Basil Blackwell, Oxford.

P. K. Edwards (1983a) 'The Political Economy of Industrial Conflict: Britain and the US', *Economic and Industrial Democracy*, 4, pp.461-500.

P. K. Edwards (1983b) 'The Pattern of Collective Industrial Conflict', in G. S. Bain (Ed.) (1983) *Industrial Relations in Britain*, Basil Blackwell, Oxford.

P. K. Edwards (1983c) 'Control, Compliance and Conflict: Analysing Variations in the Capitalist Labour Process': paper presented to the Annual Aston/UMIST Conference on the Organization and Control of the Labour Process.

P. K. Edwards (1985) 'Managing Labour Relations Through the Recession', *Employee Relations*, 7 No. 2.

R. C. Edwards (1979) *Contested Terrain: The Transformation of the Workplace in the Twentieth Century*, Heinemann, London; Basic Books, New York.

R. C. Edwards (1981) 'The Social Relations of Production at the Point of Production', in M. Zey-Ferrell and M. Aiken (1981) *Complex Organizations: Critical Perspectives*, Scott, Foresman and Co., Illinois.

B. Ehrenreich and J. Ehrenreich (1979) 'The Professional Managerial Class', in P. Walker (Ed.) (1979) *Between Labour and Capital*, Harvester Press, Brighton.

B. Ehrenreich and D. English (1979) *For Her Own Good: Fifty Years of the Experts' Advice to Women*, Pluto Press, London.

J. E. T. Eldridge and A. D. Crombie (1974) *A Sociology of Organizations*, George Allen and Unwin, London.

A. J. Elger (1975) 'Industrial Organizations: A Processual Perspective', in J. B. McKinley (Ed.) *Processing People: Cases in Organizational Behaviour*, Holt, Rinehart and Winston, London and New York.

Employment Gazette (May 1985), Labour Force Survey: Preliminary Results for 1984.

Equal Opportunities Commission (EOC) (1981) Sixth Annual Report.

G. Esland (1980) 'Diagnosis and Therapy', in G. Esland and G. Salaman (Eds.) *The Politics of Work and Occupations*. The Open University Press, Milton Keynes.

A. Etzioni (1964) *Modern Organizations*, Prentice Hall, Englewood Cliffs, NJ.

A. Ferner (1985) 'Political Constraints and Management Strategies: The Case of Working Practices' in British Rail, *British Journal of Industrial Relations*, 23, No. 1, (March) pp.47-70.

J. Finch (1984) 'Community Care: Developing Non-Sexist Alternatives, *Critical Social Policy*, 9.

M. Forsyth (1982) *Reservicing Health*, The Adam Smith Institute, London.

M. Foucault (1979) *Discipline and Punish: The Birth of the Prison,* Penguin Books, Harmondsworth.

A. Fox (1974) *Beyond Contract: Work, Power and Trust Relations,* Faber and Faber, London.

B. Frankel (1982) 'On the State of the State: Marxist Theories of the State After Leninism, in A. Giddens and D. Held (Eds.) *Classes, Power and Conflict: Classical and Contemporary Debates,* Macmillan, London.

E. Freidson (1976) 'The Future of Professionalization', in M. Stacey *et al.* (Eds.) *Health and the Division of Labour,* Croom Helm, London.

J. Freund (1968) *The Sociology of Max Weber,* Allen Lane: The Penguin Press, London.

R. Friedland (1981) 'Central City Fiscal Strains: The Public Costs of Private Growth', *International Journal of Urban and Rural Research,* 5, pp.356-76.

A. L. Friedman (1977) *Industry and Labour,* Macmillan, London.

B. Fryer (1983) 'Managerialism, Deskilling and Trade Unionism in the Public Services': paper presented to the Annual Aston/ UMIST Conference on the Organization and Control of the Labour Process.

B. Fryer, T. Manson and P. Fairclough (1978) 'Employment and Trade Unionism in the Public Services', *Capital and Class,* 4.

A. Gamble (1986) 'The Political Economy of Freedom', in R. Levitas (Ed.) *The Ideology of the New Right,* Polity Press, Cambridge; Basil Blackwell Inc., New York.

E. Gamarnikow (1978) 'Sexual Division of Labour—the Case of Nursing', in A. Kuhn and A. M. Wolpe (Eds.) *Feminism and Materialism,* Routledge and Kegan Paul, London.

P. Georgiou (1981) 'The Goal Paradigm and Notes Towards a Counter Paradigm', in M. Zey-Ferrell and M. Aiken (1981) *Complex Organizations: Critical Perspectives,* Scott, Foresman and Co., Illinois.

J. Gershuny (1978) *After Industrial Society: The Emerging Self Service Economy,* Macmillan, London.

A. Giddens (1973) *The Class Structure of the Advanced Societies,* Hutchinson, London.

A. Giddens (1979) *Central Problems in Social Theory,* Macmillian, London.

A. Giddens (1982) *Profiles and Critiques in Social Theory,* Macmillan, London.

A. Glyn and J. Harrison (1980) *The British Economic Disaster,* Pluto Press, London.

J. Goldthorpe (1982) 'On the Service Class: Its Formation and Future', in A. Giddens and G. Mackenzie (Eds.) (1982) *Social Class and the Division of Labour*, Cambridge University Press, Cambridge and New York.

J. Goldthorpe (1985) 'The End of Convergence: Corporatist and Dualist Tendencies in Modern Western Societies', in B. Roberts, Ruth Finnegan and D. Gallie (Eds.) (1985) *New Approaches to Economic Life*, Manchester University Press, Manchester.

D. M. Gordon, R. Edwards and M. Reich (1982) *Segmented Work, Divided Workers: The Historical Transformation of Labour in the US*, Cambridge University Press, London and New York.

H. Gospel and C. R. Littler (1983) *Managerial Strategies and Industrial Relations*, Heinemann, London.

I. Gough (1979) *The Political Economy of the Welfare State*, Macmillan, London.

I. Gough (1983) 'The Crisis of the British Welfare State', *International Journal Of Health Services*, 13, No. 3.

A. Gouldner (1954) *Patterns of Industrial Bureaucracy*, Free Press, New York.

H. Graham (1983) 'Caring: A Labour of Love', in J. Finch and D. Groves (Eds.) (1983) *A Labour of Love: Women, Work and Caring*, Routledge and Kegan Paul, London.

E. Greenwood (1957) 'Attributes of a Profession', *Social Work*, 2, pp.45-55.

The Griffiths Report (1983) *NHS Management Inquiry*, DHSS.

J. Habermas (1971) 'Technology and Science as Ideology', in *Toward a Rational Society*, Heinemann, London.

J. Habermas (1976) *Legitimation Crisis*, Heinemann, London.

C. Hakim (1981) 'Job Segregation: Trends in the 1970s', *Employment Gazette*, December, pp.521-9.

S. Hall (1979) 'Drifting into a Law-and-Order Society', The Cobden Lecture 1979, The Cobden Trust, London.

C. Ham (1981) *Policy Making in the National Health Service*, Macmillan, London.

H. Hartmann (1979a) 'Capitalism, Patriarchy and Job Segregation by Sex' in Z. R. Eisenstein (ed.) (1979) *Capitalist Patriarchy and Socialist Feminism*, Monthly Review Press, New York.

H. Hartmann (1979b) 'The Unhappy Marriage of Marxism and Feminism', in *Capital and Class*, 8.

S. Haywood and A. Alaszewski (1980) *Crisis in the Health Service*, Croom Helm, London.

D. Heald (1983) *Public Expenditure: Its Defence and Reform*, Martin Robertson, Oxford.

D. Heald and G. Morris (1984) 'Why the Public Sector Unions are on the Defensive', *Personnel Management,* 16, No. 5, pp.30-4.

J. Hearn (1982) 'Notes on Patriarchy, Professionalization and the Semi-professions', *Sociology,* 16, No. 2 pp.184-202.

A. J. Heidenheimer, H. Helco and C. T. Adams (1983) *Comparative Public Policy: The Politics of Public Choice in Europe and America,* 2nd Edn. St. Martin's Press, New York (1st Edn., 1975).

D. Held (1982) 'Crisis Tendencies, Legitimation and the State' in J. B. Thompson and D. Held (Eds.) (1982) *Habermas: Critical Debates,* Macmillan, London.

D. Held (1984) 'Power and Legitimacy in Contemporary Britain' in G. McLennan, D. Held and S. Hall (Eds.) (1984) *State and Society in Contemporary Britain: A Critical Introduction,* Polity Press Cambridge; Basil Backwell, New York.

M. Henwood (1986) 'Community Care: Policy and Practice', in *The Year Book of Social Policy in Britain 1985/6,* Routledge and Kegan Paul, London and Boston.

M. Hewitt (1983) 'Bio-Politics and Social Policy: Foucault's Account of Welfare', *Theory, Culture and Society,* 2 No. 1.

S. Hill (1981) *Competition and Control at Work,* Heinemann, London.

House of Commons (1985-1986) 14th Report, Committee of Public Accounts, *Control of Nursing Manpower.*

J. Humphries (1977) 'Class Struggle and the Persistence of the Working Class Family', *Cambridge Journal of Economics,* 1, pp.241-58.

J. Humphries (1983) 'The "Emancipation" of Women in the 1970s and 1980s: From the Latent to the Floating', *Capital and Class,* 20, pp.6-28.

J. Humphries and J. Rubery (1984) 'The Reconstitution of the Supply Side of the Labour Market: The Relative Autonomy of Social Reproduction', *Cambridge Journal of Economics,* 8, pp.331-46.

J. Hunt (1980) 'Some gaps and Problems arising from Government Statistics on Women at Work', *Equal Opportunities Commission Research Bulletin,* 4.

D. Hunter (1979) *Coping With Uncertainty,* Research Studies Press, Chichester, Sussex.

I. Illich, J. McKnight, I. K. Zola, J. Caplan and H. Shaiken (1977) *The Disabling Professions,* Marion Boyars, London.

Institute of Directors (1982) *Some Thoughts on the Tasks Ahead,* London.

E. Jacques (1978) *Health Services,* Heinemann, London.

H. Jamous and B. Peloille (1970) 'Changes in the French University Hospital System', in J. A. Jackson (Ed.) (1970), *Professions and Professionalization,* Cambridge University Press, Cambridge.

B. Jessop (1979) 'Corporatism, Parliamentarism, and Social Democracy, in P. C. Schmitter and G. Lehmbruch (Eds.) *Trends towards Corporatist Intermediation,* Sage Publications, London and Beverley Hills.

T. J. Johnson (1972) *Professions and Power,* Macmillan, London.

T. J. Johnson (1977) 'The Professions in the Class Structure', in R. Scase (Ed.) (1977) *Industrial Society: Class, Cleavage and Control,* George Allen and Unwin, London.

T. J. Johnson (1980) 'Work and Power', in G. Esland and G. Salaman (Eds.) *The Politics of Work and Occupations,* The Open University Press, Milton Keynes.

L. Karpik (1981) 'Organizations, Institutions and History', in M. Zey-Ferrell and M. Aiken (1981) *Complex Organizations: Critical Perspectives,* Scott, Foresman and Co., Illinois.

E. M. Kassalow (1969) *Trade Unions and Industrial Relations: An International Comparison,* Random House, New York.

E. M. Kassalow (1977) 'Industrial Conflict and Consensus in the US and Western Europe', in *Industrial Relations Research Association Proceedings,* 30th Annual Meeting.

E. M. Kassalow (1984) 'Concession Bargaining', in ILO 1984, *Collective Bargaining: A Response to the Recession in Industrialized Market Economies,* Geneva.

J. Keane (1978) 'The Legacy of Political Economy: Thinking With and Against Claus Offe', *Canadian Journal of Political and Social Theory,* 2, No. 3.

R. C. Kearney (1984) *Labor Relations in the Public Sector,* Marcel Dekkar, Basle.

J. Kelly (1985) 'Management's Redesign of Work', in D. Knights, H. Willmott and D. Collinson (Eds.) (1985), *Job Redesign: Critical Perspectives on the Labour Process,* Gower.

J. Kendrick (1981) 'Politics and the Construction of Women as Second Class Workers', in F. Wilkinson (Ed.) *The Dynamics of Labour Market Segmentation,* Academic Press, London and New York.

C. Kerr (1954) 'The Balkanization of Labour Markets', in E. W. Baake *et al. Labour Mobility and Economic Opportunity,* Wiley, New York.

C. P. Kindleberger (1967) *Europe's Postwar Growth: The Role of Labor Supply,* Harvard University Press, Cambridge, Mass.

R. Klein (1983) *The Politics of the NHS*, Longman, London.

K. S. Koziara (1985) 'Comparable Worth: Organization Dilemmas', *Monthly Labor Review*, December, pp.13-16.

R. Kreckel (1980) 'Unequal Opportunity Structure and Labour Market Segmentation', *Sociology*, 14 No. 4.

K. Kumar (1978) *Prophecy and Progress*, Penguin Books, Harmondsworth, Middlesex.

Labour Research Department (1986) *Part Time Workers*.

Labour Research Department (May 1984) *Privatization: NHS and Laundries*, pp.113-15.

M. S. Larson (1977) *The Rise of Professionalism*, University of California Press, Berkeley, California.

M. S. Larson (1980) 'Proletarianization and Educated Labour', *Theory and Society*, 9, pp.131-75.

W. Leedham (1986) *Privatization of NHS Ancillary Services*, Workers Educational Association, London.

J. Le Grand and R. Robinson (Eds.) (1984) *Privatization and the Welfare State*. George Allen and Unwin, London and Boston.

R. Levitas (Ed.) (1986) *The Ideology of the New Right*, Polity Press, Cambridge; Basil Blackwell Inc., New York.

C. R. Littler (1982) *The Development of the Labour Process in Capitalist Societies*, Heinemann, London.

C. R. Littler (1985) 'Taylorism, Fordism and Job Design', in D. Knights, H. Willmott and D. Collinson (Eds.) (1985) *Job Redesign: Critical Perspectives on the Labour Process*, Gower, Aldershot, Hants.

C. R. Littler and G. Salaman (1982) 'Bravermania and Beyond: Recent Theories of the Labour Process, *Sociology*, 16, No. 2, pp.251-69.

K. Loewith (1970) 'Weber's Interpretation of the Bourgeois Capitalistic World in Terms of the Grinding Principle of Rationalization', in D. Wrong (Ed.) (1970) *Max Weber*, Prentice Hall. Englewood Cliffs, N.J.

London Health Emergency (1986) *Patients or Profits*.

J. B. McKinlay (Ed.) (1975) *Processing People: Cases in Organizational Behavior*, Holt, Rinehart and Winston, London and New York.

J. B. McKinlay and J. Arches (1985) 'Towards the Proletarianization of Physicians', *International Journal of Health Services*, 15 No. 2, pp.161-95.

K. McNeil (1981) 'Understanding Organizational Power: Building on the Weberian Legacy', in M. Zey-Ferrell and M. Aiken (1981)

Complex Organizations: Critical Perspectives, Scott, Foresman and Co., Illinois.

R. Mailly (1986) 'The Impact of Contracting Out in the NHS', *Employee Relations,* 8 No. 1, pp.10-16.

S. Mallet (1975) *The New Working Class,* Spokesman Books, Nottingham.

T. Mallier and M. Rosser (1979) 'The Changing Role of Women in the British Economy', *National Westminster Bank Quarterly Review,* November.

T. Manson (1976) 'Management, The Professions and the Unions', in M. Stacey *et al.* (Eds.) (1976) *Health and the Division of Labour,* Croom Helm, London.

T. Manson (1979) 'Health Policy and the Cuts', *Capital and Class,* 7.

M. Marchington and R. Armstrong (1985) 'Involving Employees Through the Recession', *Employee Relations,* 7, No. 5 pp.17-21.

T. H. Marshall (1963) 'The Recent History of Professionalism in Relation to Social Structure and Social Policy', in T. H. Marshall *Sociology at the Crossroads and other Essays* (1963), Heinemann, London.

J. Martin and C. Roberts (1984) *Women and Employment: A Lifetime Perspective,* Social Survey Report, HMSO.

K. Marx (1976) *Capital,* Vol. I, Penguin Books, Harmondsworth, Middlesex, and New York.

D. Massey (1984) *Spatial Divisions of Labour,* Macmillan, London.

M. May (1985) 'Bread Before Roses: American Working Men, Labor Unions and the Family Wage', in R. Milkman (Ed.) (1985) *Women, Work and Protest: A Century of Women's Labor History,* Routledge and Kegan Paul, Boston and London.

P. Meiksins (1986) 'Beyond the Boundary Question', *New Left Review,* 157.

A. P. Mercato (1981) 'Social Reproduction and the Basic Structure of Labour Markets', in F. Wilkinson (Ed.) (1981) *The Dynamics of Labour Market Segmentation,* Academic Press, London and New York.

G. Mercer (1984) 'Corporatist Ways in the NHS?', in M. L. Harrison (Ed.) *Corporatism and the Welfare State,* Gower.

R. K. Merton, A. P. Gray, B. Hockey and H. C. Selvin (Eds.) (1952) *Reader in Bureaucracy,* Free Press, New York.

R. Michels (1962) *Political Parties,* Collier, New York.

R. Milkman (1976) 'Women's Work and the Economic Crisis: Some Lessons of the Great Depression', *Review of Radical Political Economy,* 8 No. 1.

R. Milkman (Ed.) (1985) *Women, Work and Protest: A Century of*

Women's Labor History, Routledge and Kegan Paul, Boston and London.

G. Millerson (1964) *The Qualifying Associations: A Study in Professionalization,* Routledge and Kegan Paul, London.

D. J. B. Mitchell (1983) 'The New Climate: Implications for Research on Public Sector Wage Determination and Labor Relations', in *Labor Law Journal,* August, Chicago.

N. Mouzelis (1967) *Organization and Bureaucracy,* Routledge and Kegan Paul, London.

V. Navarro (1985) 'The 1980 and 1984 Elections and The New Deal', *International Journal of Health Services,* 15, No. 3 pp.359-94.

National Union of Public Employees (1984; 1986) Privatization Fact Sheets, Series E.

NUPE/SCAT (1985) *Private Health Care Dossier: Fines, Failures and Illegal Practices in North America.*

OECD (1985-1986) *Economic Survey USA.*

OECD Observer (1986) No. 136, March.

J. O'Connor (1973) *The Fiscal Crisis of the State,* St. Martin's Press, New York.

M. O'Higgins and A. Patterson (1985) 'The Prospects for Public Expenditure: A Disaggregate Analaysis, in R. Klein and M. O'Higgins (Eds.) (1985) *The Future of Welfare,* Basil Blackwell, Oxford and New York.

C. Offe (1972) 'Political Authority and Class Structures', in P. Connerton (Ed.) (1976) *Critical Sociology,* Penguin Books, Harmondsworth, Middlesex.

C. Offe (1975a) 'The Theory of the Capitalist State and the Problem of Policy Formation', in L. Lindberg *et al.* (Eds.) (1975) *Stress and Contradiction in Modern Capitalism,* D. Heath, Lexington, Mass.

C. Offe (1975b) 'Legitimacy versus Efficiency: Introduction to Part III, in L. Lindberg *et al.* (Eds.) (1975), *Stress and Contradiction in Modern Capitalism,* D. Heath, Lexington, Mass.

C. Offe (1976) 'Crisis of Crisis Management: Elements of a Political Crisis Theory, *International Journal of Politics,* 6, No. 3.

C. Offe (1984) 'Social Policy and the Theory of the State', in C. Offe (Ed. J. Keane) (1984) *Contradictions of the Welfare State,* Hutchinson, London.

C. Offe and V. Ronge (1975) 'Thesis on the Theory of the State', in A. Giddens and D. Held (Eds.) (1982) *Classes, Power and Conflict,* Macmillan, London.

M. Oppenheimer (1973) 'The Proletarianization of the Pofes-
sional', in P. Halmos (Ed.) *Professionalization and Social
Change*, University of Keele.

A. Pankert (1985) 'Recent Developments in Labour Relations in
the Industrialized Market Economies: Some Bench Marks',
International Labour Review, 124, No. 5, pp.531-44.
F. Parkin (1979) *Marxism and Class Theory: A Bourgeois Critique*,
Tavistock, London.
N. C. A. Parry and J. Parry (1974) 'The Teachers and Profes-
sionalism: The Failure of an Occupational Strategy', in M. Flude
and J. Ahier (1974) *Educability, Schools and Ideology*, Croom
Helm, London.
N. C. A. Parry and J. Parry (1977) 'Professionalism and Unionism:
Aspects of Class Conflict in the NHS', *Sociological Review*, 25,
pp.823-41.
N. C. A. Parry and J. Parry (1979) 'Social Work, Professionalism
and the State', in N. Parry, M. Rustin and C. Satyamurti (Eds.)
Social Work, Welfare and the State, Edward Arnold, London.
T. Parsons (1958) 'Suggestions for a Sociological Approach to the
Theory of Organizations', *Administrative Science Quarterly*, 1,
pp.63-85.
G. Peele (1984) *Revival and Reaction: The Right in Contemporary
America*, Clarendon Press, Oxford; Oxford University Press,
New York.
P. Peretz (1982) 'There Was Not a Tax Revolt', *Politics and Society*,
11, No. 2.
T. Perkins (1983) 'A New Form of Employment: A Case study of
Women's Part time Work in Coventry', in M. Evans and C,
Ungerson, *Sexual Divisions: Patterns and Processes*, Tavistock,
London.
C. Perrow (1961) 'The Analysis of Goals in Complex Organi-
zations', *American Sociological Review*, 26, pp. 854-66.
C. Perrow (1979) *Complex Organizations: A Critical Essay*, Scott,
Foreman and Co. Glenview, Illinois.
A. Phizacklea and R. Miles (1980) *Labour and Racism*, Routledge
and Kegan Paul, London and Boston.
D. Portwood and A. Fielding (1981) 'Privilege and the Professions',
Sociological Review, 29, No. 4 pp.749-73.
N. Poulantzas (1975) *Classes in Contemporary Capitalism*, New
Left Books, London.
Public Service Action No. 21 (1986) 'The Geography of NHS Pri-
vatisation', March/April, p.8, SCAT Publications, London.
Public Service Action No. 22 (1986) 'Crothalls Crisis: NHS

Managers Despair', May, p.2, SCAT Publications, London.
D. S. Pugh and D. J. Hickson (1976) *Organization Structure in its Context: The Aston Programme I,* Saxon House, London.

Radical Statistics Health Group (1987) *Facing the Figures. What is really happening in the NHS,* London, forthcoming.
G. Raynor (1982) 'The Reaganomics of Welfare: the Unfolding of the Austerity Programme', *Critical Social Policy,* 2, No. 1, pp.90-8.
G. Raynor (1983) 'Sick Hospitals: the Service Crisis of Health Care in New York City', *Critical Social Policy,* 2, No. 3, pp.46-63.
G. Raynor (1984) 'Commercial Medicine', in *Medicine in Society 1983/4,* 9, No. 4.
M. Reed (1986) 'Labour Process Theory and the Sociology of Management', paper presented to the Fourth Annual Aston/ UMIST Conference on the Organization and Control of the Labour process.
M. Reich, D. M. Gordon, and R. Edwards (1973) 'A Theory of Labor Market Segmentation, *American Economic Review,* 63 (May) pp.359-65.
M. Rein (1985) 'Women, Employment and Social Welfare', in R. Klein and M. O'Higgins (Eds.) (1985) *The Future of Welfare,* Basil Blackwell, Oxford and New York.
H. Roberts (Ed.) (1981) *Women, Health and Reproduction,* Routledge and Kegan Paul, London and Boston.
O. Robinson and J. Wallace (1984) 'Growth and Utilization of Part-time Labour in Great Britain', *Employment Gazette,* September, pp.391-7.
M. Rose and B. Jones (1985) 'Managerial Strategy and Trade Union Responses in Work Reorganization Schemes at Establishment Level', in D. Knights, H. Willmott and D. Collinson (Eds.) (1985) *Job Redesign: Critical Perspectives on the Labour Process,* Gower, Aldershot, Hants.
E. Rothschild (1981) 'Reagan and the Real America', *New York Review of Books,* 5 February, pp.12-18.
R. Rowbottom, A. Hey and D. Billis (1974) *Social Service Departments,* Heinemann, London.
D. F. Roy (1980) 'Fear Stuff, Sweet Stuff and Evil Stuff: Management's Defenses Against Unionization in the South', in T. Nichols (Ed.) (1980) *Capital and Labour,* Fontana Books, London.
J. Rubery (1978) 'Structured Labour Markets, Worker Organization and Low Pay', *Cambridge Journal of Economics,* 2, No. 1, March, pp.17-36.

J. Rubery, R. Tarling and F. Wilkinson (1984) 'Labour Market Segmentation Theory: An Alternative Framework for the Analysis of the Employment System: paper presented at the BSA Annual Conference on Work, Employment and Unemployment.

D. Rueschemeyer (1986) *Power and the Division of Labour,* Polity Press, Cambridge.

G. Salaman (1978) 'Towards a Sociology of Organization Structure', *Sociological Review,* 26, No. 3, pp. 519-54.

G. Salaman (1979) *Work Organizations: Resistance and Control,* Longman, London and New York.

G. Salaman (1982) 'Managing the Frontier of Control', in A. Giddens and G. Mckenzie (Eds.) (1982) *Social Class and the Division of Labour,* Cambridge University Press, Cambridge and New York.

G. Salaman and K. Thompson (1973) *People and Organizations,* Longman for The Open University Press, London.

G. Salaman and C. R. Littler (1984) *Class at Work,* Batsford, London.

The Salmon Report (1966) *Report of the Committee on Senior Nursing Staff Structure,* HMSO.

P. Saunders (1983) *Urban Politics: A Sociological Interpretation,* Hutchinson, London.

E. S. Savas (1982) *Privatizing the Public Sector,* Chatham House, Chatham, N.J.

M Schlesinger, R. Dorwart and R. Pulice (1986) 'Competitive Bidding and States' Purchase of Services', *Journal of Policy Analysis and Management,* 5, No. 2, pp.245-63.

P. Selznick (1949) *TVA and the Grass Roots,* University of California Press, Berkeley.

M. Shalev (1981) 'Theoretical Dilemmas and Value Analysis in Comparative Industrial Relations', in D. Glugos and K. Weirmar (Eds.) (1981) *Management Under Different Value Systems,* de Gruyter, New York.

S. Shuster (1986) 'Mortuary Attendants or Managers?', *Health Service Journal,* 3 April, p.446.

D. Silverman (1970) *The Theory of Organizations,* Heinemann, London.

J. Singleman and M. Tienda (1985) 'The Process of Occupational Change in a Service Society: The Case of the US 1960-1980', in B. Roberts, Ruth Finnegan and D. Gallie (Eds.) (1985) *New Approaches to Economic Life,* Manchester University Press, Manchester.

T. Skocpol (1980) 'Political Response to Capitalist Crisis: Neo-

Marxist Theories of the State and the Case of the New Deal',
Politics and Society, 10 No. 2.

G. Smith (1970) *Social Work and the Sociology of Organizations,*
Routledge and Kegan Paul, London.

G. Smith (1980) *Social Need: Policy, Practice and Research,* Routledge and Kegan Paul, London.

D. Soskice (1984) 'Industrial Relations and the British Economy',
Industrial Relations, 23, No. 3.

B. Spencer (1985) 'Shop Steward Resistance in the Recession',
Employee Relations, 7 No. 5, pp.22-8.

D. Stark (1982) 'Class Struggle and the Transformation of the
Labour Process: A Relational Approach', in A. Giddens and D.
Held (Eds.) (1982) *Classes, Power and Conflict: Classical and
Contemporary Debates,* Macmillan, London.

A. L. Stinchcombe (1959) 'Bureaucratic and Craft Administration
of Production', *Administrative Science Quarterly,* 4.

J. Storey (1983) *Managerial Prerogative and the Question of
Control,* Routledge and Kegan Paul, London and Boston.

J. Storey (1985) 'The Means of Management Control', *Sociology,*
19, No. 2, pp.193-211.

A. Strauss (1978) *Negotiation: Varieties, Contexts, Processes and
Social Order,* Jossey-Bass, San Francisco.

A. Strauss, I, Schatzman, R. Bucher, D. Ehrlich and M. Satshin
(1963) 'The Hospital and its Negotiated Order', in E. Friedson
(Ed.) *The Hospital in Modern Society,* Free Press, Chicago.

W. K. Tabb (1978) 'The New York Fiscal Crisis' in W. K. Tabb and
L. Sawyers (Eds.) *Marxism and the Metropolis,* Oxford University Press, New York.

P. Taylor-Gooby (1985) *Public Opinion, Ideology and State
Welfare,* Routledge and Kegan Paul, Boston and London.

M. Terry (1983) 'Shop Steward Development and Management
Strategies', in G. S. Bain (Ed.) *Industrial Relations in Britain,*
Basil Blackwell, Oxford.

A. W. J. Thompson and P. B. Beaumont (1978) *Public Sector
Bargaining: A Study of Relative Gain,* Saxon House, Farn-
borough, Hants.

P. Thompson (1983) *The Nature of Work: An Introduction to
Debates on the Labour Process,* Macmillain, London.

P. Thompson (1986) 'Crawling from the Wreckage: Labour Process
and the Politics of Production': paper presented to the Fourth
Annual Aston/UMIST Conference on the Organization and
Control of the Labour Process.

K. Thurley and S. Wood (Eds.) (1982) *Industrial Relations and*

Management Strategy, Cambridge University Press, Cambridge and New York.

The Tribune Group (1985) *The Welfare State Under the Tories: A Skeleton Service*, Tribune, London.

G. Tullock (1976) *The Vote Motive*, Institute of Economic Affairs, London.

B. S. Turner (1981) *For Weber*, Routledge and Kegan Paul, London.

C. Ungerson (Ed.) (1985) *Women and Social Policy*, Macmillan, London.

J. Urry (1983) 'Deindustrialization, Classes and Politics', in R. King (Ed.) (1983) *Capital and Politics*, Routledge and Kegan Paul, London and Boston.

S. Walby (1985) 'Approaches to the Study of Gender Relations in Unemployment and Employment', in B. Roberts, Ruth Finnegan and D. Gallie (Eds.) (1985) *New Approaches to Economic Life*, Manchester University Press, Manchester.

A. Walker (1984) 'The Political Economy of Privatization', in J. Le Grand and R. Robertson (Eds.) *Privatization and the Welfare State*, George Allen and Unwin, London and Boston.

K. Walsh (1982) 'Local Government Militancy in Britain and the United States', *Local Government Studies*, November/December, pp.1-18.

K. Walsh (1985) 'Workforce', in S. Ranson, G. Jones and K. Walsh (Eds.) (1985) *Between Centre and Locality*, George Allen and Unwin, London and Boston.

M. Wardell (1986) 'Labor and Labor Process': paper presented to the Fourth Annual Aston/UMIST Conference on the Organization and Control of the Labour Process.

A. Webb and G. Wistow (Eds.) (1982) *Whither State Welfare?*, Royal Institute of Public Administration, London.

A. Webb and G. Wistow (Eds.) (1985) 'Social Services' in S. Ranson, G. Jones and K. Walsh (1985) *Between Centre and Locality*, George Allen and Unwin, London and Boston.

M. Weber (1947) *The Theory of Social and Economic Organizations*, Edited with an Introduction by T. Parsons, The Free Press, New York; Collier-Macmillan, London.

M. Weber (1948) 'Science as a Vocation', in H.·H. Gerth and C. W. Mills (Eds.) (1948) *From Max Weber*, Routledge and Kegan Paul, London.

M. Weber (1968) *Economy and Society*, Bedminster Press, New York.

B. Webster (1985) 'A Women's Issue: The Impact of Local Authority Cuts', *Local Government Studies,* March/April.

K. Weddell (1986) 'Privatizing Social Services in the USA', *Social Policy and Administration,* 20, No. 1, pp.14-27.

J. W. Weiss (1981) 'The Historical and Political Perspective on Organizations of Lucien Karpik', in M. Zey-Ferrell and M. Aiken (1981), *Complex Organizations: Critical Perspectives,* Scott Foresman and Co., Illinois.

C. Whittington and P. Bellaby (1979) 'The Reasons for Hierarchy in Social Service Departments: A Critique of Elliot Jacques and His Associates', *Sociological Review,* 27, No. 3.

P. Wilding (1982) *Professional Power and Social Welfare,* Routledge and Kegan Paul, London.

H. Willmott (1985) 'Dialectic Analysis, Labour Process and the State': paper presented to the Third Annual Aston/UMIST Conference on the Organization and Control of the Labour Process.

A. Witz (1984) 'Patriarchy and the Labour Market: Occupational Control Strategies in the Medical Profession': paper presented to the Second Annual Aston/UMIST Conference on the Organization and Control of the Labour Process.

S. Wood (Ed.) (1982) *The Degradation of Work? Skill, Deskilling and the Labour Process,* Hutchinson, London.

S. Wood and J. Kelly (1982) 'Taylorism, Responsible Autonomy and Management Strategy', in S. Wood (Ed.) (1982) *The Degradation of Work? Skill, Deskilling and the Labour Process,* Hutchinson, London.

E. O. Wright (1976) 'Class Boundaries in Advanced Capitalist Societies, *New Left Review,* 98.

E. O. Wright (1985) *Classes,* Verso Books, London.

D. Wrong (Ed.) (1970) *Max Weber,* Prentice Hall, Englewood Cliffs, N.J.

M. Zey-Ferrell and M. Aiken (1981) *Complex Organizations: Critical Perspectives,* Scott, Foresman and Co., Illinois.

D. H. Zimmerman (1969) 'Record Keeping and the Intake Process in a Public Welfare Agency', in S. Wheeler (Ed.) *On Record: Files and Dossiers in American Life,* Russell Sage Foundation, New York.

Author Index

Subject Index